The
EXECUTION OF MAYOR YIN
and
Other Stories

THE EXECUTION OF MAYOR YIN

and Other Stories from the Great Proletarian Cultural Revolution

Revised Edition

CHEN RUOXI

Edited by Howard Goldblatt

With a new introduction by Perry Link

Translated from the Chinese by Nancy Ing
and Howard Goldblatt

INDIANA UNIVERSITY PRESS
BLOOMINGTON AND INDIANAPOLIS

This book is a publication of

Indiana University Press
601 North Morton Street
Bloomington, IN 47404-3797 USA

http://iupress.indiana.edu

Telephone orders 800-842-6796
Fax orders 812-855-7931
Orders by e-mail iuporder@indiana.edu

Library of Congress Cataloging-in-Publication Data
Chen, Ruoxi.
[Short stories. English. Selections]
The execution of mayor Yin and other stories from the great proletarian Cultural Revolution / Chen Ruoxi ; edited by Howard Goldblatt ; with a new introduction by Perry Link ; translated from the Chinese by Nancy Ing and Howard Goldblatt. — Rev. ed.
p. cm.
ISBN 0-253-34416-6 (cloth : alk. paper) — ISBN 0-253-21690-7 (pbk. : alk. paper)
1. Chen, Ruoxi—Translations into English. 2. China—History—Cultural Revolution, 1966–1976—Fiction. I. Ing, Nancy. II. Goldblatt, Howard, date III. Title.
PL2840.J6A6 2004
895.1'352—dc22
2004000689

1 2 3 4 5   09 08 07 06 05 04

For those who suffered because of the Revolution

CONTENTS

Editor's Preface to the Revised Edition

A quarter of a century ago, when *The Execution of Mayor Yin* first appeared, it comprised a significant part of what Western readers knew about Mao's Cultural Revolution, which ended in 1976. We now know much more about what happened over that hellish decade, and why; but for anyone wanting to know what it was like to live in a society gone terribly wrong, Chen Ruoxi's finely crafted stories remain the best place to start. The call to issue a new edition is proof that this view is shared by others.

I was pleased to have been asked to undertake a modest revision of the work on behalf of Nancy Ing, who initiated the project and translated most of the stories. The most obvious changes include the conversion of English spellings of Chinese names and terms to the pinyin system, except for several widely recognized names, and the deletion of some of the footnotes. Stylistic improvements have been kept to a minimum.

We are grateful to Perry Link for his willingness to introduce this new edition, and to Simon Leys, whose introduction graced the pages of the earlier edition. As before, the author's support has made this all possible.

Introduction to the Revised Edition

Perry Link

When an editor at Indiana University Press told me that the press planned to re-publish Chen Ruoxi's "Mayor Yin" stories, the idea immediately felt good. Indeed there was something strange about how good it felt. Why, I wondered, are these stories still so important? In the mid-1970s, when they first appeared, the excitement about them was easier to understand: they were then unique windows into a mysterious China; they were also among the first signs the outside world had of the catastrophic failure of the Maoist experiments of the 1950s and 1960s. Later, however, there was a flood of writing on such themes. In the late 1970s, "scar" literature, followed in the 1980s by works of "reflection" and "root seeking," turned Chen Ruoxi's early trickle of truth into a broad tide. Criticism of the Mao years, which rose to a crescendo in the 1980s, became so commonplace that by the 1990s many writers considered it passé. So haven't the "Mayor Yin" stories been superceded?

No, oddly. They continue to stand out, and for reasons other than their having been chronologically first. They stand out because no Chinese writing has yet exceeded them in looking squarely at the heart of the Maoist calamity.

It is not easy to "look squarely" at disaster in one's national past. Shock, pain, confusion, and shame can all erect barriers. As other cases in the twentieth century make clear, the effort to look and to come to terms can take time—or, more precisely, can require the psychological distance that passage of time can provide. Anne Frank wrote a diary during the Holocaust, recording what she saw, heard, and thought in her immediate environment, but "Holocaust literature" of a kind that looks at history, that tries to see it squarely, to encompass it, to understand the un-understandable and somehow to "come to terms," took decades to appear. Primo Levi's writing, which began as a survivor's notes about a death camp in the 1940s, reached its maturity, indeed achieved a remarkable poetic grace, in 1986 with *The Drowned and the Saved*.* Aleksandr Solzhenitsyn and Vaclav Havel not only exposed political prisons in Soviet Russia and Czechoslovakia but helped their readers to address moral issues that an entire oppressive system thrust before them. In Japan, "Atomic Bomb Literature" has sought to absorb the disasters of August 6 and August 9, 1944, into the Japanese national psyche, but again, although poems and witness accounts appeared soon after the bombs fell, the kind of humanist transcendence that suggests Primo Levi—and had, moreover, to understand Japan as both aggressor and victim—came only with Oe Kenzaburō's *Hiroshima Notes* in 1965,† while relatively full literary address of the devastation awaited Ibuse Masuji's *Black Rain* the following year.‡ Pol Pot's killing fields in Cambodia during 1975–79 are recorded in several literary memoirs, but, as yet, only rarely do these show enough regaining of balance to address the unfathomable questions of "How could it

---

I sommersi e i salvati (Torino: Einaudi, 1986); translated by Raymond Rosenthal as *The Drowned and the Saved* (New York: Summit Books, 1988).

†*Hiroshima nōto* (Tokyo: Iwanami shoten, 1965); translated by Toshi Yonezawa as *Hiroshima Notes*, ed. David L. Swain (Tokyo: YMCA Press, 1981).

‡*Kuroi ame* (Tokyo: Shinchōsha, 1966); translated by John Bester as *Black Rain* (Tokyo and Palo Alto: Kodansha International, 1969).

happen?" and "What does it mean?"* In South Africa, the protracted disaster of apartheid has provided several writers time to reflect and to try to comprehend, and some have done it well, but none quickly.

The human disasters just noted are of course incomparable in many ways. They involve genocide, class warfare, world warfare, empire and colonialism in complex and differing patterns. But human recoil from extremity also has its commonalities, and to ignore these might be as big a mistake as to ignore all the historical differences. So let me proceed, with caution, to suggest three broad commonalities: 1) human societies seek psychological recovery from disasters, 2) literary expression can play an important role in this effort, and 3) the passage of time seems important in gaining perspective. By these measures China's Maoist disasters—primarily the Great Leap Forward and the Great Proletarian Cultural Revolution—present some awkward questions: Is China able to look squarely at the worst of what occurred? Is the culture seeking to interpret those facts and "come to terms"? What are writers doing to help?

The Mao nightmare continues to haunt China's modern self-conception and subtly to undermine its national self-respect. Those frightening times loom in the not-so-distant background like a fetid fog that neither dissipates nor forms itself into a cloud coherent enough to be named and understood. And, inside China, the problem is not just with the past but with its extension into the present: the collapse of Mao's promises to China left the country with a deep public cynicism that has hardly diminished through the ensuing years. It is true

---

*Parts of Someth May's autobiography, *Cambodian Witness,* ed. James Fenton (London and Boston: Faber and Faber, 1986), achieve remarkable perspective.

that in today's China the spirit of money-making diverts attention from past troubles, especially among the young; but the prevalence of deceit and corruption in public life and the ruthless competition to gain advantage at any cost show that China has yet to recover from the disillusionment that Mao caused, from the sting of realizing that "Serve the People" turned out to be a fraud. All of this calls for literary address. The saga of Maoism in China is certainly enough to allow hope that a Chinese Primo Levi, Oe Kenzaburō, or Vaclav Havel might appear, but so far none has. Time of course is necessary; but it has been nearly thirty years since the beginnings of the unraveling of Maoism, and thirty years should be enough. It is sad, and for a Sinophile like me even a bit embarrassing, to look through China's voluminous literary output of the past three decades and have to admit that, for an honest look at Mao's subversion of Chinese life, nothing appears to have gone much beyond those first, limpid sketches by Chen Ruoxi. The reasons for this lack are worth exploring.

Soon after Mao's death "scar literature," led by Lu Xinhua's story "Scar,"* uncovered recent patterns of official hypocrisy and corruption and showed how politics had devastated family and social life. Nearly all problems were attributed only to a "Gang of Four and its followers," and there were clear limits on how much unpleasantness one could put down on paper. You could say Red Guards "struggled" people, but not that they gouged their eyes out; you could mention Mao, but not implicate him. Still, the opportunity for public discussion of Mao-

---

*"Shanghen" *Wenhuibao* (Shanghai), August 11, 1978; translated by Bennett Lee as "The Wounded," in Lu Xinhua et al., *The Wounded: New Stories of the Cultural Revolution, 77–78,* trans. Geremie Barmé and Bennett Lee (Hong Kong: Joint Publishing, 1979).

era pain was so exhilarating, and had been bottled up for so long, that public enthusiasm for scar literature skyrocketed. The circulations of literary magazines reached levels that have not been matched before or since. The appetite for national self-examination was strong. It was just the kind of trend that might, if left alone, have led to a mature "coming to terms" with China's Maoist episode.

For several reasons this did not happen. First, the prohibition against criticizing the Communist Party, although constant through the Communist years, proved to be especially debilitating to scar literature because it not only ruled certain comments out of bounds but had a distorting effect on nearly everything that did get into print. The underlying spirit of scar writing was to protest the basic direction that China had taken in recent years. Yet writers could target only miscreant officials—not the Party, the system, or the current top leadership. One had to say or imply—or at least allow it to be reasonably inferred—that the original system was sound and the current top leadership clean. This requirement induced in scar writing a pervasive attitude of supplication. *If only* the true path of socialism had been followed, *if only* Zhou Enlai could have lived longer and done more, *if only* intellectuals had been seen as sincerely patriotic, etc., then the catastrophes would not have happened—and, therefore, we the writers of scar literature appeal to you in the leadership to keep the rudder of the Party in the right direction from now on. In a number of works, such as Wang Meng's *Bolshevik Salute*,* this "supplicatory attitude" was the main point, and was set out explicitly. Yet in a larger

---

*"Buli," *Dangdai*, March 1979: 4–39; translated by Wendy Larson as *Bolshevik Salute* (Seattle: University of Washington Press, 1989).

sense supplication underlay virtually all of scar literature. It did not have to be forced upon writers; many of them actively sought re-acceptance by a chastened Party. In Chen Rong's *At Middle Age*,* no censor required that a Party Secretary send a car to pick up the heroine from the hospital at the story's end. The author said she wanted it that way; appreciation of intellectuals had not been a pattern in recent Chinese life, and she was appealing that it now become one.† Other writers added "happy tails" to their stories perhaps less willingly, but few broke out of the pervasive mode of supplication. For a reading public that stood in need of a thorough, probing look at the Maoist debacle, this approach had obvious limitations. (Chen Ruoxi, who was grounded in a different context, was quite free from it. She did not need to appeal to the Party and did not even think of doing so. More on this below.)

A second problem in the "scar" era was that even the limited freedom that writers had was trimmed back beginning in 1980, less than three years after it had arisen. Deng Xiaoping had needed a public outcry in order to justify his sharp turn away from aspects of Maoism, so for a time scar literature had served his purposes. But once his policy departures were secure, any deeper probing by Chinese writers would only have undermined his own regime, and so were dangerous, and so were repressed. Writers were told to stop exposing social problems and to join hands with the public at large to "look forward"—neither to pardon the past nor to condemn it, but just to let it go, to pretend it did not matter, to set it aside and to concentrate on the future. It is hard to imagine any guideline

---

*"Ren dao zhongnian," *Shouhuo* 1980.1: 52–92; translated by Yu Fanqin and Wang Mingjie in Shen [Chen] Rong, *At Middle Age* (Beijing: Panda Books, 1987), pp. 9–85.
†Interview with Chen Rong, August 7, 1980, Beijing.

that could contradict more directly a writer's effort to "look squarely" at a national disaster or try to interpret it. In addition to the intrinsic difficulties of such a project, now there were government penalties for even trying. Most Chinese writers, whether willingly or not, bent under this wind—and this, I believe, is the main reason why, in all the vastness of ink on paper that has appeared in China since the early 1980s, there is not much to rival the work of Chen Ruoxi. We cannot survey everything here, but let us look at some examples—each of which, in a different way, illustrates the problem of coming to terms with the Maoist past.

Zhang Xianliang has written tens of times—maybe a hundred times—as many words as Chen Ruoxi, and is justly famous for revealing life and psychology in Maoist labor camps.* No Chinese writer, in my view, has done more than Zhang to examine the daily grind of camp life and the ways in which hunger, thirst, deprivation of sex, isolation from family, and enforced mendacity can affect a person's mental life. On these topics Zhang is in a league with Someth May writing about Pol Pot's camps, or Bloke Modisane evoking South African township life,† and even, although without the poetry, Primo Levi recalling the Holocaust. But Zhang differs from these writers, and from Chen Ruoxi, in his conceptual frame. He grounds himself in a fundamental loyalty to the system "before it went wrong." He seems (at least until his neocapitalist turn of the last

---

*Especially in his later novels such as *Xiguan siwang* (Taipei: Yuanshen chubanshe, 1989), translated by Martha Avery as *Getting Used to Dying* (New York: Harper Collins, 1991); *Fannao jiushi zhihui* (Vexation is wisdom) (Beijing: Zuojia chubanshe, 1994), abridged and translated by Martha Avery as *Grass Soup* (London: Secker & Warburg, 1994); and *Wo de puti shu* (Beijing: Zuojia chubanshe, 1994), translated by Martha Avery as *My Bodhi Tree* (London: Secker & Warburg, 1996).
†*Blame Me on History* (New York, Dutton, 1963).

ten years or so) to feel profoundly guilty about his Shanghai-banker family background and to wish, against all the evidence that he himself provides, that there truly had been, or could be, a "revolution" of the kind that his ideals have called for. Chen Ruoxi does not carry such baggage. Moreover, she writes better than Zhang, who, although an astute observer of human psychology, is not a literary artist. Yang Jiang, who has also written about the Mao camps,* is considerably more graceful, but Chen Ruoxi's best work exceeds even Yang's. In its artful structure, evocative language, and generation of an almost excruciating poignancy, "Geng Er in Beijing," in my view, is one of the best stories in all of modern Chinese literature.

In a way very different from Zhang Xianliang's, the fractured narrative and violent descriptions of "experimentalist" writers who appeared in the late 1980s—Can Xue, Yu Hua, Han Shaogong, Bei Cun, and others—also seem to suggest a recoil from Mao. Where, we might wonder, were these writers inspired to write such unsettling unpleasantness as Can Xue's "The Things That Happened to Me in that World"† or Yu Hua's "One Kind of Reality"?‡ Some had read Western "absurdists" (Franz Kafka), or "magical realists" (Gabriel García Márquez), and others. But they had also grown up during China's Mao-madness, had sometimes been literally orphaned by politics, and as children had been even less ready than adults

---

*Yang Jiang, "Ganxiao liuji" (Six chapters on cadre school), *Guangjiaojing* (Hong Kong), no. 103 (April 1981), translated by Howard Goldblatt as *Six Chapters from My Life "Downunder"* (Seattle: University of Washington Press, 1983).

†"Wo zai neige shijieli de shiqing," *Renmin wenxue*, November 1986: 92–94, translated by Ronald R. Janssen and Jian Zhang in *Dialogues in Paradise* (Evanston, Ill.: Northwestern University Press, 1989).

‡"Xianshi yi zhong," *Beijing wenxue*, 1988.1: 4–25, translated by Jeanne Tai as "One Kind of Reality," in *Running Wild: New Chinese Writers*, ed. David Der-wei Wang with Jeanne Tai (New York: Columbia University Press, 1994), pp. 21–68.

for "rational" understanding of the bizarre cruelty that surrounded them. Perhaps no one, including the Chinese experimentalists themselves, can precisely trace their jarring writing to its roots (whose possibilities, by the way, are not limited to those I have just mentioned). But if, and insofar as, their upset does indeed stem from Mao experience, it can only be a first step in any larger cultural quest to "come to terms" with a national past. Can Xue's stories give us interesting pictures—and perhaps highly accurate ones—of mental phenomena that might be ripples from her own childhood trauma. But to move from those impressions toward a public understanding that can be useful in national recovery is a tall order.

Yet another way to look back at the Maoist past is in the ultra-direct style of Zheng Yi. Zheng is best known for his 1984 story *Old Well*,* a middle-length work of fiction set in a rocky village in Shanxi and later made into a prize-winning film. But in another vein of his writing, Zheng makes "facing up" his top priority. To authorities and to ordinary citizens alike, he seems driven to say, "*Look at this,* dammit, even if you don't want to!" In 1979, when writers were encouraged to attack the Gang of Four without showing physical violence directly, Zheng Yi effectively said, "No, I am going to show physical violence directly." His story "Maple,"† about Red Guards killing one another, barely could be published (and an illustrated version was indeed stopped by postal censors). In the mid-1980s Zheng got wind of reports that, in parts of Guangxi

---

Lao jing (Taipei: Hai feng chubanshe, 1991). English translation by David Kwan, *Old Well* (San Francisco: China Books, 1989).
†"Feng," *Wenhuibao*, February 11, 1979; translated by Douglas Spelman in *Stubborn Weeds, Popular and Controversial Chinese Literature after the Cultural Revolution,* ed. Perry Link (Bloomington: Indiana University Press, 1983), pp. 58–73.

in 1968, Maoist fervor had reached the hideous height of inducing ritualized cannibalism. The ultimate sign of triumph over the "class enemy" became the act of consuming some of the enemy's body parts after killing him. Zheng sought counsel from Liu Binyan, the distinguished writer of literary reportage, and learned that Liu—although he had also heard of these reports, and found them credible—had decided not to pursue them. The story was "just too ugly," Liu felt. But to Zheng it was not; he continued to feel a mission to seek out precisely the most ugly facts, the ones that defined the limits of how far things had gone wrong, and to force himself and his compatriots to face them. He traveled to Guangxi, where, from interviews and archives, he found solid evidence of sixty-four cases of political cannibalism. He then took three years to write them up, in careful detail and with much ancillary comment, in a 686-page book called *Red Memorial*.* If the world had a prize for the "squarest look" at disaster, it is hard to see how any book would beat this one.

Still, in terms of helping Chinese culture as a whole to come to terms with the past, *Red Memorial* has not achieved much. The book was banned inside China. But even underground (where other banned books have thrived), and even outside China where it is available in bookstores, *Red Memorial* has not circulated too well. Some of the reasons are not hard to see. It remains difficult—as with the A-bomb, the Holocaust, and elsewhere—to look at those things that are "just too ugly." But this is only part of the problem. Worries over national "face," exacerbated by a sense of a history of humiliation over the last

---

Hongse jinianbei (Taipei: Huashi wenhua gongsi, 1993); abridged and translated by T. P. Sym (pseud.) as *Scarlet Memorial* (Boulder, Colo.: Westview Press, 1996).

two centuries in encounters with the West, lead many Chinese to fear that a book like Zheng's will cause foreigners to form negative opinions not just of Maoism but of Chinese culture and all Chinese people. In the 1990s China's leaders deliberately stimulated nationalism in order to recoup their battered legitimacy after the 1989 Beijing massacre had brought it to a low, but this whipped-up nationalism is not what I mean here. The reaction to *Red Memorial* was grounded at a deeper level. Even liberal intellectuals feared that Zheng's book, when read by foreigners, could do more harm than good. The question led to spirited debate in literary circles, with Liu Binyan and others favoring publication, but equally eminent figures, such as the literary critic Liu Zaifu, demurring. No one doubted the truth of Zheng Yi's reports. The question was whether the nation's shame should be exposed to the world.

The examples above, ranging from Zhang Xianliang to Can Xue to Zheng Yi, show very different kinds of responses to Maoism. I have chosen them with this variety in mind, because the variety itself helps to illustrate how difficult it has been for Chinese writers, no matter how they come at Mao, actually to "get there"—actually to help their fellow Chinese take a square look. It's as if a huge reverse magnet were lodged at the heart of the Mao period; various literary attempts all take aim, then gather speed, then are somehow deflected. The value of Chen Ruoxi's stories is that they are not deflected; they do get there. She describes the suffering of ordinary people without, at any level, needing to supplicate a still-reigning political authority. She uses plain, undistorted language, with no need to leave readers guessing about where violence fits in. And, as an overseas Chinese, she has other places to invest her national pride than in the "face" of a brutal government. (Here, though, we must give special credit to Chen; not every overseas Chinese can see the wisdom of this simple point. It is far too common that, in looking for something on which to pin their national pride, overseas Chinese look past all the splendors of China's history, philosophy, poetry, painting, calligraphy, food, etc. and opt for a dilapidated political regime to be their emblem.) In short, the art of Chen's "Mayor Yin" stories, had she continued to write in their vein, might have matured into something much fuller. I will not chide Chen for failing to become "the Chinese Primo Levi" or "the Chinese Vaclav Havel," because her literary art is unique and would certainly have continued to differ from that of others had she gone on. And, of course, her decision of what route to take through life belongs to her, not to a cheering bystander, however sincere. I dare to mention my thought only because she herself does. In an e-mail to me in summer, 2003, she writes that, "Now, I . . . wish that I had done more, i.e., written more and better." Yes, I want to reply. Yes, and all of China might have been better off if you had.

Chen Ruoxi's stories are referred to in English as "fiction," but the term can be misleading. They are not spun from imagination, curious though some of their details might seem. In Chinese they are called *xiaoshuo*, or writing about "small" affairs, which traditionally meant stories about love, family life and the passions and problems in ordinary people's lives, which stood in implicit contrast to *dashu*, or the "great" stories about emperors, ministers, generals, and the other events that were worthy of historical records. In contemporary terms, Richard Nixon's visit to China was a great story, while accounts of how ordinary citizens were obliged to dismantle their clothes-drying racks in order to prettify an apartment building in anticipation of Nixon's visit ("Nixon's Press Corps," below) were *xiaoshuo*. But both kinds of writing were *true*—or, if embellished here and there, at least largely true. The essential distinction between them was not that of fiction and non-fiction.

Hence the "Mayor Yin" stories should be read as true accounts. In the mid-1960s Chen Ruoxi and her husband, who were originally from Taiwan but had gone to the U.S. for graduate study, joined political movements among left-wing overseas Chinese students. In 1966 they made the courageous decision to put their ideals into practice and headed to China to support the Chinese revolution and to serve the people. From 1966 until 1973 they lived in Beijing and Nanjing, where they endured, and watched others endure, the brunt of Mao's Great Proletarian Cultural Revolution. What they saw and heard of daily life indeed brought revolutionary change to their outlook, but not of the kind they had anticipated. Like George Orwell, Arthur Koestler, and other socialists who admired the idea of Soviet Communism up until the point when Soviet realities kicked them in the teeth, Chen Ruoxi drew her subsequent creative energies not only from human sympathy for victims but from the sting of disillusionment at the hands, to borrow Koestler's phrase, of "the God that failed."* Her view of Mao completely turned around, but not because her values went anywhere. Truth, civility, fairness, and human sympathy were her values throughout.

The non-fictional nature of the "Mayor Yin" stories keeps them close to the ground of daily experience, where their life-like touches are especially welcome because, in comparison

---

*Arthur Koestler et al., *The God that Failed,* ed. Richard Crossman (New York: Harper, 1949).

with other Chinese writing of the time, these touches are so rare. In the early and middle 1970s, China's published short stories, which were sometimes written by committees, could be so flat and cliché-ridden as to be almost funny, and post-Mao "scar" literature, while a big improvement, still was populated largely by one-dimensional characters. By contrast Chen Ruoxi shows us twisting, turning, surprising life. Her characters are not only three-dimensional but alive. They are the little people of Maoland—its earthworms, as it were—and, like earthworms, each squirms, and even if something slices it to bits, the bits continue to writhe. In "Residency Check" we meet Peng Yulian, cheerful and outgoing, yet apparently an adulteress, and in any case the target of a vicious rumor barrage. We also meet her husband, the broken victim of a political campaign, aged before his time and not a good match for his vivacious wife. He is victimized by her adultery and its attendant public scorn, but he forgives her, and she in turn decides to continue supporting him, and life proceeds. We see as well inside the story's narrator, who, reminiscent of Lu Xun's narrators,* shares with us the moral dilemmas of how I, the bystander, should react to all of this. Chen's narrators afford a blanket sympathy toward all earthworms, yet the moral dilemmas they present are also very real.

In following her characters through life, Chen treads across political "forbidden zones" as if they were not there. ("Scar" writers could not do this. They did "break into" forbidden areas, but were usually very self-conscious about doing so, pre-

---

*For example, in "Guxiang" (My Old Home) in *Nahan* and "Zhufu" (The New Year's Sacrifice), and "Zai Jiuloushang" (In the Tavern) in *Panghuang;* translated by Yang Xianyi and Gladys Yang in *The Complete Stories of Lu Xun* (Bloomington: Indiana University Press, 1981), pp. 55–65, 153–183.

paring in advance for both battle with opponents and the cheers of supporters.) Chen treats it as no big deal to tell us, for example, about Mayor Yin's KMT (Nationalist) background even when this background shows that the Communist armies of the 1940s acted more treacherously than the KMT's. Her story called "Ren Xiulan" is pretty much out-of-bounds from start to finish. Ren Xiulan was a Party secretary whose ultra-leftist "May 16th Group" lost out in an arcane political struggle at the top; she was therefore detained as a counterrevolutionary and held under 24-hour surveillance, from which she eventually "escaped," after which everyone in the College of Hydraulic Engineering where she had worked, including the small schoolchildren, was mobilized to hunt her down. In the end her body was discovered rotting in a cesspool into which she had thrown herself.

We do not know what the Communist Party's Department of Propaganda, behind its closed doors in the mid-1970s, said specifically about "Ren Xiulan" or others of Chen's stories, but here are some reasonable guesses: classic poisonous weeds, a crop of blatantly anti-socialist anti-Chinese slander, the frenzied jottings of an active counterrevolutionary who had slithered her way into the midst of the people. What, though, to do about it? Ban the stories inside China, of course; then, in the outside world organize some "patriotic" overseas Chinese to expose the author as a bourgeois interloper. Invite some of these patriotic guests to China, bring them to the College of Hydraulic Engineering in Nanjing to hear that Chen Ruoxi is a snake, and then send them back to spread this message abroad. One writer who accepted such an invitation, but whose name I will withhold, went to Nanjing with the aim of uncovering the actual people upon whom Chen's stories were based. This writer's plan made sense. By meeting the actual people, she could easily measure and then demonstrate Chen's class biases and unpatriotic motives. Life surprised her, though. According to an eyewitness at a seminar that she held with Chen Ruoxi's former colleagues, she seemed uneasy at hearing even more of the grisly details connected to the Ren Xiulan story. In a final effort to break through the fictional level and get at the truth, she asked, "What was Ren Xiulan's real name?" When the answer came back "Ren Xiulan," she seemed stunned. The story was *xiaoshuo,* but not fiction. There had been no fabrication, no embroidery, no obvious class bias. What happened happened. Ren Xiulan was Ren Xiulan. The seminar ended.

When Chen's stories appeared in the 1970s, it was becoming fashionable in Chinese literary studies in the West to decry "reflection of life" as a literary ideal. This fashion, while unfortunate, had understandable causes. For many years China-watchers had been using Chinese fiction to get a "picture of life" in a society where other accesses to daily experience were almost impossible to get. To literary scholars this kind of naïve-realist use of art by social scientists was almost as frustrating as the naïve art itself. Chinese writers themselves, moreover, had long labored under the enforced guideline to "reflect social reality," and now, in the late 1970s, when some were trying to break free of this stricture, Western literary scholars naturally sympathized. Finally, scholars' theoretical musings on the role of language were beginning to call into question what exactly is meant by "reflection" in the first place. But none of this should have justified the rather extreme result that ensued. Scholars, critics, and eventually some Chinese writers as well, began to assume that ordinary life should have no role in art and that in order to be "artistic" a literary work needed to stress technique alone or adventure into the fantastic. The precedents of twentieth-century masters like Lu Xun or Shen Congwen (in whose stories there is no contradiction between "life" and "technique"—both are there) were temporarily set aside. Chen Ruoxi would have gotten more critical acclaim in the 1970s and 1980s if the field had not been marching in a different direction.

Knowing that Chen's sketches are true stories makes them more moving, not less. Our sympathy for actual victims, whom we can imagine actually tracing, is only part of this response; it comes as well from feeling that the stories are "true to life"—meaning life in general—in that magnified sense that good art can achieve. Chen's artistic technique is unobtrusive. Critics have called her writing "simple," which is fair enough if "simple" means unpretentious or inornate. But the simplicity is far from artless.

Consider her unsentimental *bidiao*, or literary "tone." Here, too, she stands in contrast to most of her near-contemporaries, the "scar" writers, who spilled emotion onto their pages as if there were no tomorrow (which, given the uncertainty of Chinese literary politics, may not have been a bad calculation from their point of view). Chen understands that the impact on the reader is most powerful not when a narrator wails "this is tragic, weep for it!" or "this is outrageous, shout at it!" but when she sets out key points, with parsimony, and lets the reader infer the terrible impact on his or her own. When the long-suffering Mayor Yin is about to be shot, for example, he shouts "Long live Chairman Mao," causing his executioners, fingers on triggers, to feel a curious dilemma: to shoot the criminal is required, but to "open fire on such slogans"* is unthinkable. Here a lesser writer—including most "scar" writers—would likely have expatiated: Imagine equating a human life with slogans!

---

*"The Execution of Mayor Yin," p. 32 of this volume.

Just look at this distortion of values, of language, of life! *Wu-hu-ai-zai*! But Chen Ruoxi's narrator is brief: here is what I saw; here is what I heard. The reader must do some of the work of inferring the horror of the scene, but that work itself involves the reader more deeply and so creates a greater impact. At the end of "Geng Er in Beijing," the iron-terse dialogue between the parting lovers is almost unbearable in the emotion it packs, and yet none leaks out. The tragedy of Geng Er's wasted life rises to transcendence.

Occasionally Chen Ruoxi's flourishes resemble Lu Xun's. She ends her Geng Er story with "the sputter of exploding firecrackers and the gleeful shouts of children" in a way that recalls Lu Xun's close of his Xianglin Sao saga with "the ceaseless explosion of crackers in the distance . . . preparing to give Luzhen's people boundless good fortune."* Geng Er's languid mood of regret over hotpot and wine recalls the similar retrospection, over hot *doufu* and wine, in "In the Tavern." At a deeper level, Chen's writing resembles the best work of Lu Xun's disciple Xiao Hong, who had the same ability to use graceful and deceptively "simple" prose to tell you, without comment, or need of comment, facts that blow your hat off.†

Lu Xun and Chen Ruoxi both use irony, but of different kinds. Lu Xun's narrators sometimes stray from a straight account of things (any reader knows that Xianglin Sao's death was hardly "boundless good fortune"), leaving the reader to choose whether the narrator is sarcastic or unspeakably callous. Chen's narrators, by contrast, reliably report what they see, hear, and feel. They may do this artfully—from different points

---

*"The New-Year Sacrifice," in *The Complete Stories of Lu Xun*, p. 171, note 17.
†See "Hulanhe zhuan," translated by Howard Goldblatt as *Tales of Hulan River* (Boston: Cheng & Tsui, 2002).

of view or out of chronological order—but there is never a distance between what they say and what they mean. Chen's irony is the "situational" kind: it inheres in life itself, and is generated by the distance between what gets described and what a reasonable reader might expect. For example, in "Jingjing's Birthday," a mother knows that if her child accidentally soils an image of the Chairman her whole family can be ruined, so she takes the precaution of not buying any books that bear the Chairman's likeness. In other words the power of the Chairman is so penetrating that it prevents the spread of materials designed to spread the power of the Chairman. Chen's narrator does not invent this irony, or even spell it out. The telling is artful, requiring some reflection from the reader in order to be seen in its nudity. Sometimes Chen's irony pervades a story, stretching across several pages and imparting something close to humor. What, for example, does the entire city of Nanjing do to prepare for the possible arrival of reporters who might or might not accompany Richard Nixon who might or might not visit the city? Take down all its drying racks, of course. Here, too, Chen's writing departs from most "scar" fiction, which on the whole is too sentimental to be so wry.

I have noted above that Chen Ruoxi differs from others in that she makes no "appeal," direct or implicit, to the Communist Party. But in another direction, she does issue an appeal. Her repeated exposure of Maoist facades that are erected to deceive foreigners (a central theme of "The Big Fish" and "Nixon's Press Corps") amounts to a plea to foreigners not to be so easily deceived. She reserves special contempt for Westerners who visit China on luxurious mini-tours and then go home to help spread the lies—either because they are blinded by the romance of their privileged roles or, more darkly, because they enjoy those roles too much to risk losing them by spilling the truth. Chen names Han Suyin in this connection (in "Geng Er in Beijing"), and might have named Felix Greene, Paul Lin, or the latter-day Edgar Snow, among others. These names may seem relics from the past, sorry quirks of history that only an oddity like Maoism could have made possible. Unfortunately this is not so. Although China today is more open, and many more outsiders get better looks at more of the country, the Han Suyin syndrome remains alive and well. Whole parts of Chinese life are still tucked away from the view of foreigners, useful lies are still prettily told and naïvely accepted, overseas Chinese are still simultaneously lured by "patriotism" and threatened with cut-off from their families if they speak out, and foreign "friends of China" are still cultivated, rewarded, and cajoled. Such "friends" often end in a muddlement within which the pronouncements of top Chinese leaders and the lives of ordinary Chinese people can somehow become hard to distinguish—a malady for which a professorship in political science is not, alas, necessarily an antidote. It would be wonderful if the outside world no longer needed to hear Chen Ruoxi's appeal, but it does.

Chen makes her point about Han Suyin in her normal way— by showing, not telling. In clear, spare prose she relates an anecdote about Han and leaves the irony and disgust for the reader to figure out. Clear, spare writing is naturally powerful, of course, but many observers have noted that an authoritarian context magnifies this effect. To ban a bit of truth can turn it into a brick, or, as Simon Leys noted in his 1978 introduction to the first edition of this book, "In the empire of lies, the humblest truth is revolutionary."* And a web of lies not only has the odd effect of enhancing the value of truth; it simultaneously constricts itself by the need to maintain a crafted pretense. Vaclav Havel has noted that the Czech regime of the 1970s was "captive to its own lies" and thus always had to pretend. "It pretends to persecute no one. It pretends to fear nothing. It pretends to pretend nothing."† And it needed, of course, to guard the appearance of consistency among its pretenses.

How does such a system handle an obdurate plain-speaker like Chen Ruoxi? The fact that the Chinese government's Chen Ruoxi problem has not melted away during a quarter century of "reform and opening" is one more piece of evidence that essential features of the political system have been continuous from Mao Zedong to Hu Jintao. Chinese government views on Chen Ruoxi have flipped and flopped. Confrontation has alternated with cajolement. In the late 1970s the regime banned Chen's work and tried to discredit it. For two years she was on a visa blacklist. In the early 1980s Party General Secretary Hu Yaobang decided that Chen was "patriotic" after all and invited her to China. She visited in 1984, and in the late 1980s was again regularly published in Guangzhou and other Chinese cities, although her Cultural Revolution pieces remained under ban. In 1989, after she denounced the Tiananmen Massacre, she was again banned and blacklisted. (What did they expect from her? one wonders. A Brent Scowcroft, ready to dine with the architects of the massacre in order to preserve good relations?) In 1993 the visa ban was lifted, but not the ban on her writing, which remains in place today.

---

*Introduction to *The Execution of Mayor Yin*, p. xxi.
†Vaclav Havel, "The Power of the Powerless," in *Living in Truth* (London and Boston: Faber and Faber, 1989), p. 45.

In any context, when one party's judgments of another change as fitfully as this, we have to suspect that somebody, either the judging side or the side that is judged, is confused, or perhaps even has lost bearings. Which side might that be? Is Chen Ruoxi flopping about, trying this and trying that, looking for what works? Or is it a frightened government in Beijing that is still groping, still wondering if Ren Xiulan is Ren Xiulan, still pretending to pretend nothing?

The
EXECUTION OF MAYOR YIN
and
Other Stories

The Execution of Mayor Yin

Mayor Yin and I met only twice, but I shall never forget him.

In the fall of 1966 I went to Xi'an from Beijing and stayed at the home of my friend, Lao Wu, or "old" Wu. His only son, Xiao Wu, "little" Wu, was one of those arrogant Red Guards who, despite the fact that he was only a second-year high school student, exhibited an air of authority, loudly proclaiming such revolutionary slogans as "Support Chairman Mao" and "Rebellion is right and just."

He could not bear to take off his olive-green uniform long enough for it to be laundered, so his collar and cuffs were always shiny with oily grime. But his red armband was bright and clean, and whenever he met anyone he would stand with his right hand on his hip, forcing people to recognize the authority that five-inch-wide band of dazzling red silk represented. He and another Red Guard were preparing to set off for Xing'an County in southern Shaanxi province to kindle the fire of rebellion there. The spirit of revolution lagged in that backward area, which did not even have a Red Guard organization, so Xi'an's Red Guard Headquarters decided to send two competent cadremen to set up operations.

Xiao Wu volunteered for the job. He was originally from Xing'an and had moved to the provincial capital with his parents when he was twelve years old. He could thus serve the revolution and also revisit his old home and see his friends and relatives. Both private and public interests could be served. Of course, it was taboo to speak of "serving private and public interests," since that was the time of the slogan "Down with private interests; serve only the public good." This sort of thing simply invited criticism. One had to base all personal conduct on Mao Zedong's teachings: "Never think of yourself; think only of others."

It happened that I had just completed my official mission and did not have to report back to Beijing for almost two weeks. On a former assignment I had visited all the famous scenic spots of Xi'an, such as the Great and Small Wild Goose Pagodas, the Forest of Monuments, and the artifacts from the diggings of Banbianpo. Since I had nothing better to do around there, I accepted Lao Wu's suggestion that I accompany his son and a schoolmate to southern Shaanxi to take in the sights of the Hanzhong Basin.

It took us a day and a night by bus to cross the peaks of the Qinling Mountains and reach Xing'an. All along the way it was mountain after mountain, and the bus was forever tilting to one side. I was constantly dizzy and a little nauseated, and even when I got off at the station I felt that I leaned as I walked. The Qinling Mountains are like a massive screen, and the scenery changed completely from the northern to the southern slopes. When we left Xi'an it was already late autumn, and the trees were bare, the grass a withered brown; but in Xing'an the land was green as far as the eye could see, as if one had found oneself south of the Yangtze River.

Xiao Wu arranged for me to stay at the home of his relative, Lao Yin, while he and his schoolmate went to stay at the county middle school dormitory. Lao Yin was past seventy, but he was still strong and hearty. His wife had died the year before, so he lived all alone in a large one-room brick house, which he kept meticulously neat and clean. He seemed genuinely happy to accommodate a guest from afar. As soon as we stepped inside the door he cheerfully put aside his long pipe, rolled up his sleeves, and began to cook. Xiao Wu and his friend, in the tradition of the Liberation Army, laid down their packs and started to chop firewood and carry water from the well.

After dinner, just as Xiao Wu and his friend were about to leave for the dormitory, a bespectacled man in a cadre uniform strode into the room. When Xiao Wu saw him he hesitated a moment before reluctantly addressing him as Uncle. Then he introduced us, saying, "This is a distant uncle of mine," stressing the word "distant."

We did not know the visitor's name, so both Xiao Wu's schoolmate and I very politely followed suit in addressing him as Uncle. As soon as he finished with the introductions, Xiao Wu hurriedly grabbed my hand to look at my wristwatch. "It's late," he exclaimed, "and I'm afraid the student dormitory will close." In obvious haste, he urged his friend to get ready, then picked up his pack and left with him.

This uncle of Xiao Wu's seemed surprised and nonplussed by their sudden departure. While greeting us warmly his eyes continued to gaze with wonder at Xiao Wu's red armband. He was a very tall man, dark and thin, about fifty years old. His back was straight and strong, suggesting that he must have presented an impressive figure in his youth. He looked you straight in the eye, and when he listened he bent his head slightly as if afraid to miss a single word. The expression on his face was diffident and gentle. He wore a neat gray tunic, which everyone called a Mao jacket, cotton socks and shoes, showing him to be a typical old cadreman from any part of China, north or south.

He sat down, and after exchanging amenities with Lao Yin, turned and asked me courteously who I was. Upon hearing that I was on a sightseeing visit to southern Shaanxi, he seemed more relaxed and expressed his welcome. He spoke with the sincere diffidence of the midlander. "Our Xing'an is a back-ward, out-of-the-way place. Aside from this boundless chain of Qinling Mountains and Daba Mountain, there's only the Han River. However, in the mountains to the north there are some waterfalls that are worth seeing. It's too bad that at the moment we're again involved with a campaign that makes it impossible for me to get away, or I'd be happy to escort you there."

Maybe the word "campaign" reminded him of something, for his face darkened and he sighed softly. Lao Yin turned on the room's single light bulb and brought him a cup of hot water, but he didn't drink it. He just sat for a while in silence, then got up and left.

The next day hospitable Lao Yin got up early in the morning to cook some rice porridge, breaking his habit of many years of eating only two meals a day. I was much refreshed after a good night's sleep and suddenly remembered the cured pork and dried beef I had bought in Xi'an. I hastened to offer them to Lao Yin. As we ate our porridge I mentioned "Uncle" and learned that he was the mayor of Xing'an. His surname was also Yin, and thus he was a kinsman of Lao Yin.

"He was commended for his meritorious service during the Revolution and became the acting mayor. After Liberation he continued to serve as a member of the district committee, but everyone continued to address him as Mayor Yin," said Lao Yin.

It turned out that Mayor Yin had been an officer under the Kuomintang general Hu Zongnan, and with thousands of soldiers under his command, he had guarded a strategic pass along the southeastern edge of the Qinling Mountains. Since it would have been almost impossible to take the pass by force, underground Communist agents had been sent to work on subverting Colonel Yin's loyalty. At the time he was a young man in his twenties who commanded the allegiance of his soldiers, men recruited from the area around the Qinling Mountains, so when he resolutely threw down his arms and went over to the Communists, his troops followed him.

"And so, without wasting a single bullet, the red flag began to fly over three counties in southern Shaanxi."

As he finished talking Lao Yin lit his long pipe and took several vigorous puffs on it, blowing out the smoke slowly. His old eyes twinkled, as if the memories of the past could still stir his emotions. Since I have always respected those who could see a situation clearly, discerning what is right from what is wrong, I too applauded Mayor Yin's wisdom.

"I'm not trying to paint a flattering picture of him just because he's a kinsman of mine—you can ask anyone who lives within forty *li* of here. When he went over to the other side he wasn't seeking personal wealth or position; he only asked for a guarantee of safety for his soldiers, and that they be given the chance to reform and make a new start. I don't think there are many Kuomintang officers who could have behaved like that!"

"There certainly weren't many like that," I agreed.

"Nowadays it's those who come from a good background who have the advantage. During the land reform period the working committee in his village classified his old mother as a poor peasant. But he actually requested that her status be changed, since when his father was alive they'd often hired laborers to help out at the busiest times on the farm, and according to government policy, that would classify them as rich peasants. In the end they put her down as a middle peasant."

"Well, that shows that Mayor Yin was pretty radical!"

"Hm, you don't know the half of it. During the 1951 Three Antis and Five Antis campaigns* he was the only cadreman in the county who came out unscathed. Even the Party Committee secretary was changed several times. As I recall, it was during those campaigns that the first one was dismissed for being corrupt."

"How could they change the secretary of the Party Committee so many times?" I was somewhat taken aback by this remark.

"Ai, the situation in our county was complicated, mainly because the peasants couldn't keep up with the constant political changes in politics. So production suffered. When the

---

*The Three Antis campaign (*sanfan yundong*) was directed against corruption, waste, and bureaucratism; the Five Antis campaign (*wufan yundong*) was aimed at bribery, evasion of taxes, theft of state property, skimping on work and cheating on materials, and theft of state economic information.

rate of production failed to increase, other problems developed, and since these problems could not be solved, they got rid of the secretary. To tell the truth, ever since Liberation, production has improved and our lives have gotten a little better, though we still cannot compare with the people in the midlands. You've just come from there and you know that in those eight hundred *li* along the Qin River the harvest from one season can last for two years. The situation isn't bad here, but it's much worse in the smaller areas. Whenever there are periods of bad weather, famine still occurs and people are reduced to eating leaves and grass and the bark of trees. A few years back during a bad harvest I went to my old home in the mountains. My neighbor's daughter could not come out to greet me, for she had no trousers to wear. Her mother had exchanged their cloth coupon for food. This is just between you and me, and I trust you won't turn around and brand me a counterrevolutionary."

I shook my head solemnly. "I'm not a Party member, and besides, I detest those who report on people behind their backs."

Lao Yin spat contemptuously, expressing his agreement.

"There were plenty of hardships here during those three years. But in all fairness, I've lived more than seventy years, and I've seen worse times than these before Liberation. In those days people not only sold their children, there were even cases of cannibalism. During the recent period of bad times, the cadres were just as hungry as everyone else, so the people were placated by firing the Party secretary. The Communists acknowledge their mistakes, and for that I respect them. And in a way it's fortunate that these three years have been so difficult, or else Mayor Yin would've fallen long ago."

"Why, did he do something wrong?"

"He spoke out a few times during the Hundred Flowers period,* and in fact he led the criticism of the agricultural policies. Who would have guessed that there would suddenly be an anti-rightist campaign and that he would almost get a rightist label hung on him? His wife, who'd been working in the county, was transferred, and if it hadn't been for Mayor Yin's meritorious service, she would've been sent to the caves in northern Shaanxi. They had plans to make him a Party member and he'd already made application, but this anti-rightist campaign spoiled everything. Actually, he never wanted to become a Party member anyway. He once told me that never in his life would he be able to master the theories of Marxism.

"After the campaign was launched it was rumored that he would be stripped of his committee membership and dismissed from his position as mayor. But in the spring and summer of 1960 we were plagued with the worst drought we'd ever had, and not a single kernel of corn or wheat was harvested. The peasants' morale was very low, and there were many grain robberies. Even the grain sent by the government for famine relief couldn't solve the problem. So they were not only unable to dismiss Mayor Yin, they had to delegate to him the responsibility for handling agricultural production. During those two years he personally went into the villages and called on the peasants to keep up production. At the same time he relaxed regulations and encouraged the peasants to exert themselves to the utmost. He allowed them to retain small plots of land for private use and permitted them a little more freedom in order

---

*A campaign for freer criticism of the cadres and bureaucracy begun in 1956 under the slogan "Let a hundred flowers bloom together, let the hundred schools of thought contend." The outpouring of criticism by intellectuals led to an anti-rightist campaign intended to stifle all criticism.

to stimulate self-interest and establish a common market for free trade . . ."

"Aiya, Uncle Yin," I couldn't keep from interrupting him, "there you go, bringing up that Three Freedoms and One Contract affair!* You should know that the aim of the Cultural Revolution is to discover who was responsible for that fiasco. The wall posters in Beijing are already hinting at Liu Shaoqi, without mentioning names, and urging that this restoration of imperialist policies be soundly criticized!"

"Is that true?" The old man stared at me.

"Of course it's true!" I lowered my voice. "I heard many people saying so with my own ears."

"I'm getting so old I can't keep up with things." As he shook his head in discouragement the few white hairs on his forehead quivered. Suddenly his attitude hardened again and he knitted his brow so tightly that his face looked like a withered orange. "I don't understand," he said angrily. "Wouldn't the peasants have revolted if he hadn't done what he did?"

"Don't talk like that!" I warned him hastily. "If your relative did carry out this policy, then he won't be able to escape being criticized and condemned."

The old man began to laugh, saying with a careless shrug: "So what? Public criticism is common fare for the cadres, and even little fry like me have been publicly criticized countless times over the past few years."

"You're right. They say that this time the purpose is to oppose and guard against revisionism. Our main task is to dig up the roots of Liu Shaoqi's revisionist policies. As to the people

---

*(Sanzi yibao.) The Three Freedoms were extension of plots of land for private production, free markets, and increase of private enterprise. The One Contract was a contracted obligation by each household for producing a fixed quantity of grain.

who merely carried out his policies, they will only undergo thought reform."

"That's as it should be," the old man agreed, somewhat mollified. "When Mayor Yin was pushing that Three Freedoms and One Contract way of thinking he was only following orders from above. How could he have invented something like that himself? Ever since the anti-rightist campaign he has been County Committee chairman in name only."

Although his mind seemed clear on the matter now, Lao Yin became preoccupied, remaining silent and thoughtful. When he was not busy he would sit on a small stool in the doorway smoking his long pipe, his eyes blinking nervously as though he were troubled.

Things really moved fast after that. In the two days since I'd last seen Xiao Wu, large red and green posters had appeared in the small county town, announcing the establishment of a local Red Guard organization. They called on all citizens and students to rise up and join in the revolution, pointedly urging all political cadremen to purify themselves by fire and carry out their revolutionary duties voluntarily.

The main thoroughfare of the town was the east–west highway. Lao Yin's house was at the west end, and standing on tiptoe by the side of the road looking eastward, I could see all the most important buildings in town: the county high school, the elementary school, and the movie theater at the farthest end; the County Committee office, the department store, and the bus station in the middle; and the county hospital near the west end. During those few days I often saw middle school students with brushes and pails full of paste, which they smeared on the walls with bold strokes before sticking up the large posters. Peasants going into town on business stood around watching curiously, the younger ones even pointing as they exchanged comments. Occasionally the people's attention was captured by the noise of a motor, as a small tractor would come down from the mountains, filled with many enthusiastic, windblown faces. As soon as they had passed, everyone's eyes would turn back to the huge black letters and the rousing slogans of the posters:

DRAG OUT THE CAPITALIST ROADER XXX!

WE SHALL FIGHT ANYONE WHO TRIES TO COVER UP!

XXX MUST BOW DOWN AND CONFESS HIS GUILT!

XX, YOUR CRIMES HAVE BEEN FOUND OUT. YOUR

DAYS ARE NUMBERED!

SHAANXI RED COMMAND AND XING'AN REVOLUTIONARY

GROUP, MARCH FORWARD COURAGEOUSLY!

On the streets people could be heard loudly discussing the accusations against the Party secretary. The Red Guards wanted to hold a big meeting to criticize and denounce him for resisting the Sixteen Points,* for sabotaging the campaign, and for corruption. They even threatened to parade him through the streets! Then just as the campaign reached its peak, a large new poster suddenly appeared on the main gate of the county elementary school denouncing another cadreman. I walked over to take a look at it, but the crowd was three or four deep, so it took me some time to work my way up to the poster.

The heading read: "Who is the Real Class Enemy?" Beneath it was a smaller caption: "Beware of Catching the Small Shrimps and Letting the Big Fish Slip Away!" It urged

---

*The sixteen points (*shiliu tiao*) adopted by the eleventh plenum of the Central Committee of the Chinese Communist Party on August 8, 1966 for the purpose of regulating the activities of the Red Guard.

the people to drag out the real class enemy from the County Committee, the underworld criminal, the warlord of the Kuomintang era. It stated that he had masqueraded as a radical, lied about his background, and habitually fleeced the people, and that his landlord-class wife had resisted any and all kinds of reformation, and so on. At first I didn't know whom this referred to, but when I heard the people around me discussing the matter, it was clear that it was aimed at Mayor Yin. The flames had finally reached his head. Although I realized that the situation was inevitable and was dictated by the course of events, I heaved a sigh nonetheless.

After dinner that evening Xiao Wu came to see me, bringing a bus ticket to Hanzhong for the next day. I mentioned the poster I had seen that day and casually asked him what the problem was with his "Mayor Uncle."

On hearing the word "Uncle" his face turned bright red, and his nostrils twitched with indignation. He began to grumble about the difficulties of organizing work, complaining that the mountain youths were backward and stubborn and had no understanding whatsoever of policies. The newly organized revolutionary corps, it turned out, had been manipulated by someone in the background who, without warning, called for first purging the mayor and then arresting the Party secretary.

"This must be the work of Liu Shaoqi's running dogs," Xiao Wu said as he ground his teeth. "They want to protect those heading down the capitalist road, so they've changed the direction of the campaign and begun striking an already dying dog."

"Why? Is your uncle a veteran of political campaigns?" I quizzed Xiao Wu.

He shrugged his shoulders. "At most he is only a rightist who has slipped through the net. My uncle . . ."

At this point he stopped abruptly and shook his head vigorously, as though he had made up his mind to disavow the family relationship.

"Everyone knows that Yin Feilong has been the mayor in name only these many years. To go after him with all this fanfare is straying far from the main path. This is nothing short of catching the small shrimp and letting the big fish slip away. That Party secretary is rotten and corrupt, and he behaves immorally with women. The people were really angered, yet they let him go so easily. I suspect he's the one in the background who is manipulating some of the Red Guards and creating this split. But when I suggested that we go after the real culprit, there were some who accused me of trying to shield my own relative. Their mothers' . . . !"

He grew angrier as he talked, so full of resentment that he could not sit still on the bench. Suddenly he stood up and pounded his fist on the dining table, almost breaking the dishes. I was startled and did not know how to comfort him. I glanced at Lao Yin. He blinked his eyes indifferently as he smoked his long pipe. Occasionally he would look coldly at Xiao Wu without saying a word.

As soon as the sun set behind the mountain, the wind began to rise. It became stronger and louder. Afraid of being caught in a storm, Xiao Wu refused to stay any longer; he turned up his collar and hurried off. Lao Yin turned on the light and cleared the dining table. He boiled some water and then banked the fire, while I packed a bag for the next day's trip.

By the time we finished washing up it was nine-thirty, a time when most people in this mountain city had already retired. Just as we were about to turn out the light and get into bed, there was a very soft knock on the door. Lao Yin was sitting on the edge of the bed, bending over to take off his shoes, and apparently hadn't heard it. Wondering who it could be, I unbolted the door. A figure slipped in with the wind, and quickly closed the door behind him. In the light of the swaying lamp I could see that it was Mayor Yin. His coming to call at this late hour took me completely by surprise.

He apologized for disturbing us. "It isn't often that I have a chance to meet a comrade from Beijing, so I couldn't refrain from asking you a few questions."

I invited him to sit at the table. Lao Yin pulled his shoes on and came over to join us. Mayor Yin removed his cap and glasses; and probably because he did not know where to begin, he took out his handkerchief and concentrated on polishing his glasses. His bronzed face, appearing larger than usual without his glasses, was overshadowed with fatigue and uncertainty. We were sitting very close to one another, and I noticed a scar under the corner of his left eye that stretched across to his ear. There was also an inch-long surgical scar on the back of his right hand. I surmised that they stemmed from his days as a soldier. Except for these marks, it would be impossible to imagine him now as the "warlord" the large posters accused him of being. I didn't know whether he was aware that his name had been posted, and I couldn't bring myself to ask him.

He remained silent for a moment, then suddenly looked directly at me and came right to the point: "Just why are we having this Cultural Revolution?"

From the note of urgency in his voice I could easily imagine his turbulent state of mind. And yet at that moment I myself was unclear as to the actual significance and purpose of the Cultural Revolution. I could only recite to him all the familiar statements that I had read in the papers and heard in various discussions.

The more he listened, the more puzzled he seemed to grow; his head leaned far to one side; his brows were tightly knit.

"I still don't see what this Cultural Revolution has to do with me." He waited until I had finished my stock response before he continued, carefully putting his glasses back on. "I've never been the leader in this county—not even the second in command. I've never been involved with organization, propaganda work, or any policy making. Whatever the Party told me to do, I did. I only have one head, which the Party can reform any way it wishes to. As for my family history, I've already reported it five or six times since Liberation. What's there to cover up, to lie about?"

He mumbled the last sentence to himself, and as he finished talking he bent his head, supporting it with his right hand. The scar on the back of his hand looked like a vine from which the grapes had been plucked clean; it glowed red under the light.

Neither Lao Yin nor I knew what to say. My host coughed dryly, reached into his pocket for matches, and mechanically lit his beloved pipe, which was already a shiny black from a lifetime of use.

I pulled out a pack of Front Gate cigarettes and offered it to Mayor Yin, but he shook his head and said that he didn't smoke. I lit one for myself as I tried to console him. I urged him to have faith in the policies of the Party and the people, and above all to believe in Chairman Mao's doctrine of "criticizing severely but sentencing leniently." By the time my cigarette had burned all the way down, my mouth was dry from talking. If I had continued I would have said nothing but lies.

He listened attentively, nodding his head now and then, although he could not hide a slightly bitter smile. "I'm not worried about myself," he declared frankly. "This is the only good thing about having no children. But I have feelings of regret, though I don't quite know why. It's as though I've never done anything, never contributed anything to the nation, to the people."

"You mustn't think too much," I said. "None of us must think too much. As long as each one of us does his best, we're contributing to the welfare of the country."

But he smiled sadly as he shook his head in disagreement. "When I first heard about Communism I was almost thirty years old. At that time I wasn't at all clear whether the Communist ideals would ever be realized, or what it would be like if they were. I believed only that they were better than Sun Yat-sen's doctrine of the Three Principles of the People. The Communists' style was superior to that of the Kuomintang, and Mao Zedong was better than Chiang Kai-shek—Chiang Kai-shek made no real effort to resist the Japanese.

"It's too bad I found out about it too late. I was inducted into the army when I was fifteen and I experienced so many hardships. I was interested only in my own survival and how I could climb up and become the commander of a regiment, then a division, and eventually become a general. My only thoughts were of myself. So when someone told me that the Communists wanted to teach people to live for others and to work for the common people of China, I began to feel how insignificant and unclean I was. I felt that my life had been empty, that I had lived in vain. I remember I was once so moved that my hands began to sweat until the horse whip in my hand was dripping wet.

"But after all, I come from a lowly background and didn't have much book learning as a child, so even though after Liberation I joined several study groups, my level of culture was too low. I never could understand the doctrines of Marxism. I sometimes believe that their books were written only for the intellectuals, or that they weren't meant for the Chinese people in the first place. Before the anti-rightist campaign the local Party organization directed me to study Liu Shaoqi's *How to Be a Good Communist,* and I seemed to gain something from that. After all, he speaks our language. Now we've been directed to learn the teachings of Chairman Mao. A few days ago we brought out several dusty volumes of his works from the storeroom."

I told him that Liu Shaoqi had been forced to step aside and that his *How to Be a Good Communist* was considered poison because he had quoted sayings from Confucius and Mencius. Mayor Yin was completely dumbfounded by this news.

"What's wrong with Confucius and Mencius?" he asked. "I once studied an article by Chairman Mao that also had quotations from Confucius and Mencius!"

"When Chairman Mao uses them that's different, of course," I said matter-of-factly. "But when other people use them it's with the ulterior motive of serving their counter-revolutionary aims."

Since I wasn't much clearer on this point than he, I hurriedly changed the subject. "Why were there discrepancies in the two reports you made about your family background?"

At this he stared at me as though he were being held forcibly by someone who would not let go.

"I did report falsely," he acknowledged frankly, his face filled with contrition. "Not long after I'd gone over to the Communists I was placed in a study group where we studied the policy of leniency toward prisoners of war. The cadre called on the people to be truthful, to empty their hearts. There was one man who took the lead in approaching the Party, and the sins he confessed were truly frightening. Execution by a firing squad would have been too light a sentence to hand down, but he was forgiven. We officers who had surrendered were moved to tears.

"Everyone fought to be the first to go to the Party cadre to talk, to confess, to empty his heart. It was as though the more evil our pasts contained, the more glorious we'd become. I was even sorry then that my father wasn't a warlord or a secret police officer! So when I filled out the forms I wrote 'landlord.' It was at least believable, since who didn't believe that all of Chiang Kai-shek's officers came from the tyrannical landlord class?

"During the land reform campaign in 1953 the working committee in my village classified my family as poor peasant, because at the time of Liberation my family had no land at all. We'd had some land at first, but in 1948 it had been given to my sister as her dowry. My parents lived on what I sent them, which was much more than they could earn from farming. At that time I felt that being classified as poor peasants was in fact not being truthful to the Party. My father had died, so I wrote to the Party secretary of the county, asking that we be classified as rich peasants. Afterward, the county notified my mother that she had been changed to upper middle peasant. In fact, it was my brother-in-law who later suffered from this, since he was classified as a rich peasant because of the added farmland. So he became a member of the Black Five* This added burden caused trouble between him and his wife, and affected their marriage."

---

*The Black Five (*hei wulei*) were landlords, rich peasants, counterrevolutionaries, bad elements, and rightists.

His voice gradually grew hoarse and finally died away, leaving behind only a tragic smile. I could find no words to comfort him and merely heaved a deep sigh.

"It's getting late." This was the first time Lao Yin had opened his mouth. He'd put aside his long pipe and was sitting there with his arms folded, looking worriedly at Mayor Yin.

The wind had died down a bit, but now the pattering of the rain could be heard, sounding like spring silkworms chewing mulberry leaves. Mayor Yin stood up as though he had just awakened from a dream, put on his cap, and muttered something incoherent. Lao Yin kept shaking his head as we saw him to the door. Lao Yin offered him the umbrella by the door but he refused and strode out. We watched his tall figure disappear in the wind and rain, into the darkness of the night. Lao Yin bolted the door and turned out the light, and in silence we groped our way to bed.

The next day I left for Hanzhong.

I returned to Xing'an a week later. It was sunset, and the mountain peaks, the trees, and the houses were all bathed in brilliant gold. The bus station was plastered with posters in large characters and brightly colored cartoons and propaganda pictures, so dazzling to the eye that one did not know where to look. With my bag in hand I strolled around the small waiting room. One look at the headlines and I knew that Mayor Yin had become the target.

I went over to the county middle school to take a look at the posters there. As I passed by the door of the theater I saw that the movie advertisements had been papered over with huge slogans. The notice "Closed in order to concentrate on revolutionary activities" was pasted over the ticket window. The area around the front door of the County Committee headquarters was deserted except for a middle-aged man, his back hunched over and his head bowed as he swept the steps, watched by a young fellow who was blowing smoke rings. Perhaps he was the secretary of the Party Committee, but I was not in the mood to ask questions. The street seemed livelier than it had been a few days earlier. There were more people walking back and forth, mostly middle school students in green uniforms with red armbands. The color red was everywhere: red-lettered slogans, posters in large red characters, red signboards. In the light of the setting sun they presented a scary and menacing scene. I discovered that the names of all the shops had been changed. Now there were the Red Guard Department Store, Serve the People Restaurant, Red Guard Photography Shop, Protect the East Eatery, The East Is Red Theater, and Serve the People Agricultural Equipment Repair Shop.

From a distance I could see a large crowd of people standing in front of the middle school. As I drew near I realized that a debate was going on. The crowd was so densely packed that not even a needle could be slipped into it. I had decided to turn back, but suddenly I heard a familiar voice. Whose was it? To get a good look, I stood on my bag with my back against the wall of the school. Three Red Guards were in the midst of an argument, two against one. The lone battler was a square-faced, bushy-browed youth who was obviously on the defensive. His face was fiery red, and he was cursing loudly as he mopped his brow with his handkerchief. His opponents were elated at having gained the upper hand; with heads held high, eyes bulging, and spittle flying left and right, they looked like victorious fighting cocks. The more aggressive one was none other than Xiao Wu. His face, too, was red, and his neck was thickened with shouting, but his manner was overbearing and his head was held higher than anyone else's.

"I say again," the unyielding, square-faced youth was shouting, "that we should act in accordance with the policies of the Party. Since he recanted and has served the Party well, there should be no digging into past records. That is what Chairman Mao has taught us."

"Hah!" Xiao Wu said contemptuously. "You haven't yet learned all the teachings of Chairman Mao. Chairman Mao also said that wrongs must be righted and vengeance must be exacted sooner or later. What do you say to that? Now is the time to seek revenge for our brothers!"

"You see! If he can turn against his own relative for the sake of righteousness, where do you stand?" the other one demanded fiercely.

"If one has killed then he must pay with his life. There is no other way!" Xiao Wu pressed his point.

"A blood debt must be paid in blood!" his companion shouted.

Their sentiments were echoed by some students, and although the square-faced youth continued to argue stubbornly, he was finally shouted down.

Maybe it was due to fatigue from the long journey, but I suddenly felt dizzy and nauseated. I hastily jumped down and picked up my bag. In the dying rays of the sunset, I walked toward Lao Yin's home. All along the way cries of "The killer must pay with his life" rang in my ears.

As I reached Lao Yin's doorstep the last rays of the sun died away. I was tired and hungry. All I wanted was to lie down and rest, but as I entered the house I was upset to find two guests already sitting there. A white-haired old man about Lao Yin's age was reading from a red copy of *Sayings of Chairman Mao* in such a heavy Shaanxi accent that I could not make out what he was reading. The other person was an old woman, whose eyes were glued to the little red book in her hand. She remained motionless until she heard my footsteps; then she looked up, as if she had just awakened. She stared at me in surprise, her mouth hanging slack, as though her jaw were dislocated. The old man paused for a fraction of a second as he glanced at me, then continued his reading. Lao Yin stood up from the edge of the bed, nodded at me, and sat down again. He placed the little red book on his knees and stared at its cover.

I put my bag alongside the small cot where I had slept more than a week before and went to get some water to wash up. I began to regret that I had come back to Xing'an. I could have gone directly back to Beijing from Hanzhong, but I had come back to pick up a bag I'd left behind and to buy a wooden bathtub for a friend in Beijing. How could I have known I'd arrive just when they were rectifying Lao Yin! He was in hot water, and having someone from outside the province staying at his home could only make matters worse. As I washed my face I made up my mind that I would leave immediately if transportation could be arranged.

Lao Yin came over to ladle out water to wash the rice, and then he busied himself with making a pot of rice porridge. When it was ready he placed it on the table along with a dish of pickled vegetables. The old man and woman stood up as if they had cast off a heavy burden, picked up the little stools on which they had been sitting, and left. As soon as they were out the door Lao Yin went to the cupboard and got out the bowl of Hunan smoked pork I'd brought from Xi'an.

I told him that I planned to return to Beijing the next day. He nodded. "It's best to leave this place as soon as possible." With that, he bent over to eat his porridge and didn't say a word about his own troubles.

We had just put down our bowls and chopsticks when a new team sent by those in charge of the study class came in. One was an elderly woman, the other a self-possessed woman of about forty with short hair, very much an efficient cadre member.

"Lao Yin, have you thought it over?" the younger woman asked as she pushed open the door. Her sharp eyes swept over the dishes on the table.

"I really don't know a thing," Lao Yin replied as he cleaned up the table.

"Use your head and try to remember," she said patiently. She chose the most comfortable place to sit—beside the table, with her back to the wall—and seemed prepared to stay for a long time. The old woman sat down on the other side of the table and, taking a copy of *Sayings of Chairman Mao* from her pocket, gazed fixedly at Lao Yin.

"This only happened twenty-some years ago, so why can't you remember?" the middle-aged woman continued. "Besides, he was serving under your son. So many people knew about this, how come your son never mentioned a word to you? He was only eighteen years old, so full of life, and that evil warlord Yin Feilong shot him! This is class hatred; how can you not avenge that? And how did your *own* son die? These are the accounts that the Cultural Revolution must settle."

"My son died a year before the liberation of Shaanxi," Lao Yin replied gently as he carefully wiped the table.

"How did he die? As cannon fodder for Yin Feilong! He was stubbornly anti-Communist and forced all the young boys to become cannon fodder. This is a most abominable crime! You've already reached a ripe old age, so what do you have to fear? Stand up and settle accounts with him!"

"Covering up for a relative will only add to your guilt!" The old woman also had to have her say. "Don't let his frequent visits fool you. He's like the weasel that comes to call on the chicken at New Year's time; his intentions are anything but honorable! If he has done nothing wrong, why should he try so hard to seal your mouth?"

The room was already so dark that we couldn't see each other's faces, yet Lao Yin made no move to turn on the light. He just sat silently on the edge of his bed. I was dead tired and wanted only to lie down. Finally I could hold out no longer and turned on the light. As the two women opened their books to look for a quotation, I slipped out the door and went to look for Xiao Wu.

Apparently Xiao Wu had established quite a reputation for himself, for I had no trouble locating him. He had become the deputy commander of the revolutionary corps, as well as director of propaganda. He occupied an office all by himself and had even been assigned a female secretary. On the door of his office was a new sign, "Propaganda Office: No Admittance Except on Business," written in red characters. All the lights were on, people were coming and going, and it appeared that they were prepared to work through the night.

Xiao Wu was wearing a brand new uniform with a wide leather belt. His face glowed; he was the picture of a vigorous, self-satisfied young man who has made it to the top.

I was intending to ask him why he had changed his opinion of his uncle, but the female secretary kept glaring at me. I told him only that I had to rush back to Beijing on important business and had to leave the town the next day. I asked if he could help me get transportation.

"Leave it to me," he declared as he patted his chest. "I'll let you know first thing in the morning."

In a period of less than two weeks Xiao Wu had changed a great deal. The way he talked, the way he moved, reminded me of someone delivering a speech. He was filled with self-confidence—indeed, with arrogance.

Since everything was arranged, I stood up to take my leave.

"Leaving? It's still early." He ostentatiously turned up his left sleeve and looked carefully at his new watch.

I smiled, but didn't say anything, and left the Propaganda Office to take a walk alone. The street was nearly deserted even though it was only nine o'clock; most of the stores had closed and many homes were already dark. The mountain wind was blowing and the night air was as cold as ice water. A half moon hung over the mountains; the somber, cloud-covered peaks looked like crouching beasts waiting for the chance to pounce.

Heading into the wind, I walked down the road from east to west and back again. Since all the shops were locked up, there was nothing to do but go back to Lao Yin's home. The two women were still there exhorting Lao Yin, who was sitting on the edge of the bed listening politely as he smoked his long pipe. I was so tired I couldn't stop yawning. It was almost ten o'clock. The woman who looked like a cadre member noticed me glancing at my watch, so she got to her feet, saying, "You'd better get some sleep; we'll talk again tomorrow." With that, she and the old woman quickly left.

They were, after all, mountain people, and they had genuine warmth. I was quite touched, for even though they were carrying on a reform session, they were considerate enough to let people go to bed early. In the outer provinces they often took turns interrogating from eight in the morning until late at night.

I was so exhausted that when I turned out the light and got into bed my bones ached. But before I closed my eyes I made an effort to say a few consoling words to the old man. "Lao Yin, you'd better just tell them all there is to tell. There's no night or day in their 'verbal persuasions.' They won't stop until they've achieved their goals, and why should you go through all this trouble? It's better to have faith in the Party and in the people, to clear up this matter and be done with it . . ."

My voice became lower and lower, as if I were talking to myself, and it finally died away in the darkness. After some time Lao Yin's bitter laugh broke the silence.

"But I don't know what happened. I just heard that during the war there was a soldier who disobeyed an order and Yin Feilong personally shot him. I didn't know the soldier and I didn't see it happen, so what can I say? If they want to get rid of Yin Feilong, let them go ahead and get rid of him. Why must they dig into dead issues? As for my son, he was killed fighting the Communists. What can I say?"

What could he say? This question for which there was no answer followed me into my dreams.

The next morning, to my surprise, the ingenious Xiao Wu had actually been able to procure a letter of introduction for me so that I could get on that day's flight. I was suddenly transformed into a "special observer" of the revolutionary corps and didn't even have to pay for the ticket. As the plane was taking off, Xiao Wu even came over to wave goodbye to me. I waved back through the window, but I quickly lost sight of him as the town of Xing'an disappeared into the distance. Outside the window there was only mountain after mountain, the never-ending chain of the Qinling Range.

On a windy afternoon in the spring of 1968 I was walking in Beijing's Dongdan Park when I ran into a cousin of Xiao Wu's. I'd met him only once before, in Xing'an, and it was he who recognized me and called out. He was wearing a heavy cotton padded jacket and had a bag slung over his shoulder. He was sitting on a bench peeling a pear. I was pleasantly surprised and sat down beside him to chat. He had come to Beijing with a group of Red Guards to file a complaint. The Red Guard Headquarters of Shaanxi had split into two factions, struggling with each other over the policy of "attack with reasoning and defend with force." His faction had taken the initiative of sending representatives to the capital to ask for the support of the Cultural Revolutionary Group of the Central Committee of the Communist Party.

I asked about the recent situation in Xi'an and about his uncle and cousin. "Your cousin has risen even higher, hasn't he?" I asked somewhat jokingly. "What is his position now?"

Unexpectedly, this question brought a shadow over the young man's face.

"Things have not gone well with my cousin . . ." He stammered slightly, as though he could not decide how much he should tell me. "He hasn't been back home for three months, and nobody knows where he is. My uncle is so angry with him he's developed stomach trouble."

I felt badly for my old friend when I heard this. Xiao Wu's cousin said that the two of them unfortunately were in opposing camps. Xiao Wu's group had been fiercely involved with militant tactics, and it had been publicly announced that the group leader was to be arrested. Most likely he'd gone into hiding.

"You two made yourselves entirely too conspicuous," I said bluntly. "Don't you see that times have changed? How can they let you go on rebelling? Soon the People's Liberation Army will take over. You young people just won't learn; you don't realize the importance of discipline in an organization, and you fight constantly for power and your own self-interest. If you continue like this there's little chance you'll come to any good!"

Greatly chastened by my harsh criticism of the Red Guards, he explained defensively, "We do have our faults. My uncle said the same things. This is my first trip outside of Shaanxi. I've never asserted myself in any situation, and this time I took the opportunity to come and see Beijing. I'm not like my cousin. He's gotten in too deep and can't pull himself out—his father said he let success go to his head. At the time of the execution of Mayor Yin he was so 'red' he was almost purple . . ."

"What did you say?" I interrupted him, not believing my ears. "They executed Mayor Yin?"

He nodded. "That was early in 1967."

"On what charges?" As soon as the words were out of my mouth I waved my hand. My heart was filled with despair and sorrow. "Never mind. I know what the charges must have been. As far-fetched as possible. When all is said and done, he was a revolutionary in the cause, so how could they have put him to death?"

"At the time everyone felt it was a necessary step for the sake of the revolution. If they didn't execute a few people they couldn't establish their authority and extend their influence. Afterward we all knew we'd gone too far. There were some in our faction who wanted to settle this account for him, but the time didn't seem right, so the matter was dropped. Yin Feilong wasn't the only case; there were many more like him."

As we talked a sudden gust of wind swept up pieces of paper and sand and swirled them in the air. The sun had long since been driven to some unknown place, and the desolate sky was a sheet of yellow mist. I shut my eyes tight and turned my face away from the rough wind, but this boy who had grown up on the yellow sandy highlands wasn't fazed by it. When the wind was at its strongest he even excitedly threw open his arms as if he wanted to catch hold of it. When the wind had passed he picked up where he had left off.

"I arrived in Xing'an on the day of Yin Feilong's trial. I remember that when the verdict 'Immediate execution' was announced. Mayor Yin's head fell forward. If it hadn't been for the two Red Guards behind him, who caught hold of him, he would have fainted. His wife tried to rush up to the platform, screaming all the while, 'You people follow the policy! You must follow the policy!' But she was immediately dragged away. After that the people began to cool down. Only the Red Guards around the platform clapped and shouted. My cousin jumped right up onto the platform and started shouting slogans like 'Blood debts must be paid in blood!' 'The execution of the warlord, counterrevolutionary Yin Feilong is a great victory for the thought of Mao Zedong!' At first we shouted with him, but our voices became fewer and lower. At the time I was so choked up my chest was bursting with pain. At the final shout of 'Long live Chairman Mao!' he was joined by only one voice, and it was coming from the platform. Everyone looked up—it was Yin Feilong! His arms were pinned behind him, and his glasses had fallen off, but his head was high. His face was waxen, and his eyes were staring straight ahead as he shouted over and over: 'Long live Chairman Mao! Long live Chairman Mao!' We were all stunned. The only sound was his lone voice."

"Ah . . ." I drew a long breath. My chest felt as if it would burst. I was speechless.

"As a rule, in public trials the prisoner's mouth is gagged for fear that he might shout counterrevolutionary slogans. But someone said it wasn't necessary this time, since he probably wouldn't have the nerve to do so. And then when he began to shout 'Long live Chairman Mao!' the ones holding him didn't dare cover his mouth for fear of doing the wrong thing. Then the people at the back surged toward the platform. They completely ignored the chairman of the meeting, who was calling out, 'Intensify order and revolutionary discipline!' The Red Guards rushed up onto the platform to keep the people from going up. The chairman was afraid that a riot might break out, so he quickly ordered an immediate execution. So four or five men dragged Mayor Yin out onto a truck, and without even parading him down the street, they drove directly to the rock pile. You know the place, don't you?"

I nodded. Once when I'd gone into the canyon on a cart I'd passed it—sheer cliffs on both sides of a large fan-shaped area strewn with rocks and boulders, the dried-up river bed of an old mountain stream.

"They tied Mayor Yin to a wooden stake that had been stuck in among the rocks. As they pointed their rifles at him, he raised his head and shouted again, 'Long live the Communist Party! Long live Chairman Mao!' His eyes were bulging as though they would burst from their sockets, and his lips were bleeding from biting them. Everyone was scared out of their wits. How could they open fire on such slogans? They had to stop him from shouting. My cousin had a large handkerchief, so he went up and stuffed it into his mouth. Then the executioners began to fire. This time there was no shouting, no cheers. No one wanted to go up for a closer look. The body just hung limply from the wooden stake, completely alone. I turned my head. I didn't dare look. A peasant slapped me on the back and asked, 'How could they shoot him when he was shouting "Long live Chairman Mao!" like that?'"

"What was your answer?" I asked.

He shrugged his shoulders and gave a bitter smile. "I told him to mind his own business."

We both fell silent. Another burst of wind. Dusk was falling earlier than usual.

"How is Lao Yin?" I asked.

"He's dead."

Xiao Wu's cousin said he had to attend a meeting, and hurried off. I didn't ask how Lao Yin had died, for I was reminded of the quotation from Mao Zedong that was part of our daily reading: "People die all the time."

Jingjing's Birthday*

In the beginning of September 1971 my husband wrote to me from the May Seventh Cadre School† in northern Jiangsu that his period of labor reform would soon be over. He was planning to be in Nanjing before the middle of the month, in time for Jingjing's fourth birthday on the thirteenth. He would take him out to the Sun Yat-sen Mausoleum, for as he said in his letter, "It's been three years since we came to Nanjing, and we've never gone to pay our respects to such historical monuments as the Ming Tombs and the Sun Yat-sen Mausoleum."

If he hadn't reminded me I would have forgotten all about Jingjing's birthday. Since our return to China we had even forgotten our own birthdays. For me birthdays had become a thing of the past except when my colleagues reminded me at

---

*Published in the first edition as "Chairman Mao Is a Rotten Egg."
†The May Seventh Cadre Schools (*Wuqi ganxiao*) were established throughout the country to carry out the principles of manual labor and the study of Mao's thoughts that were embodied in the May Seventh Directive (*Wuqi zhishi*), issued by Chairman Mao on May 7, 1966.

the end of each year to take my ration card and buy a catty of Strength and Prosperity Noodles—Chairman Mao's birthday noodles.

I picked up Jingjing at kindergarten, and on the way home I told him all about his father's plans. He was delighted to hear that he was going on an outing with his father, whom he hadn't seen for a long time. His little round face broke into a smile as he skipped along beside me.

Suddenly he looked up and asked, "Mommy, what's a birthday?"

"Your birthday is the day on which you were born," I answered, without giving it a thought. It was only when I saw the puzzled expression on his face that I realized the abstractness of the word "birthday." Since I was eight months pregnant at the time, I placed his hand on my swollen abdomen and said, "In another month the baby will be born, and the day it arrives will be its birthday."

I couldn't tell if he actually understood what I was saying, but he skipped ahead, shouting, "Birthday! Birthday!" I was hardly able to keep up with him, and by the time I reached the steps leading up to our dormitory area I was out of breath. Tiger Pass Dormitory, situated on a hill, consisted of several rows of one-story buildings. The families of over two hundred faculty members of the Institute of Hydraulic Engineering lived there. Our building was halfway up the hill, and climbing up and down in hot weather made me sweat profusely. Jingjing didn't stop to talk to any of his friends, but ran straight up to our quarters. "Nainai!"* he shouted happily to the old woman who had come out to meet him.

---

*Nainai actually means "grandmother," but it is also a term of respect for older women.

My neighbor, Auntie Wang, had asked the old woman to help take care of Jingjing and look after me during my confinement. Her surname was An, and she was from northern Jiangsu. She was a very straightforward person, and although we had only been together for a short while, the three of us were already on the best of terms.

"Nainai, I'm going to have a birthday. Daddy's going to take me to San San Mausoleum!"

"San San what?" An Nainai was over sixty and hard of hearing.

"The Sun Yat-sen Mausoleum," I managed to gasp as I caught up with them. I was beginning to regret having mentioned the outing to Jingjing. If he were to go around telling everyone about celebrating his birthday, people would think that his parents were still full of decadent capitalist ideas. So I quickly pulled him inside the house and told him not to mention his birthday again or one day he would become an old counterrevolutionary. He couldn't understand why he mustn't talk about his birthday, but he knew exactly what an "old counterrevolutionary" was. His face tightened immediately and he nodded gravely. I felt greatly relieved and let An Nainai take him away to wash his hands and eat his supper.

But Jingjing couldn't keep the good news to himself after all. After supper he went to Auntie Wang's to play and told Dongdong, her seven-year-old son, who was just entering the first grade. Since they lived so near us, and he and Jingjing had been together in kindergarten, they had become fast friends, playing together most of the time. Later that evening, when Auntie Wang came over to visit, the first thing she said was, "I hear that it will soon be Jingjing's birthday. Is that true?"

"Yes," I admitted with some embarrassment.

Auntie Wang was in charge of the youngest group at the kindergarten—the three- to four-year-olds—so Jingjing was in her group. Since she was very patient and sang well, the children were all very fond of her. Like so many Cantonese, she was lively and talkative. She had been designated as a poor citizen of the city (I never quite understood what this term stood for; people said that it meant an unemployed person, but I never had the nerve to question her about it), which made her one of the Five Red Elements* of society. Because of that she exuded self-confidence and spoke in a very loud voice. Evidently she regarded me favorably, as she often came over to visit in the evenings after finishing her household chores. Her husband and I belonged to the same teaching unit and at that time he was also working in the rice fields with the May Seventh Cadre School. Since we both had to look after a child in addition to going to work and doing our housework, we helped each other with shopping and other chores. If she hadn't found An Nainai for me at a time when I was still new to the place, I would have been helpless.

"Dongdong's birthday was a few days ago, on the twenty-ninth of August, but I didn't do anything to celebrate." There was an overtone of remorse in her voice. "When his daddy returns I'll ask him to take him to People's Park."

"That'll be nice," I said. "You should all go boating together in this crisp autumn weather. Just think how wonderful it would be to have a photo taken!"

"Too bad we don't have a camera."

I would have liked to lend her our Canon camera but was

---

*Children of workers, poor and lower-middle peasants, revolutionary cadres, Liberation Army men, and revolutionary martyrs.

afraid she would embarrass me by refusing my offer. So although the words were on the tip of my tongue, I said nothing. About a year earlier I had impetuously offered the camera to our Party section leader, who took one look and flatly refused it. From then on I was reluctant even to take out the camera, which had been made in a "militaristic country."

Auntie Wang couldn't stop yawning. She looked very tired, so I asked, "Didn't you get any rest today after being on duty last night?"

She shook her head as she covered her mouth with her hand. There were dark circles under her eyes.

"I lay in bed all day, but I couldn't sleep!" she said as she looked around. An Nainai was taking a bath behind the closed kitchen door and Jingjing was already in bed in the other room. She leaned over and whispered, "You know Shi Laoshi's [Teacher Shi's] daughter, Xiao Hong, don't you?"

"Of course," I said. "Isn't she in Jingjing's class?"

Xiao Hong's father and I were in the same department. He came from a choice background and had been a Party member for many years. Because of his role in the Cultural Revolution, he was now in charge of a study class to inspect the mid-level cadres in our provincial government. His wife was a teacher and was also performing labor in the May Seventh Cadre School. Since neither parent was in Nanjing, Xiao Hong was left in the care of the kindergarten day and night. She was a lovable little girl with pretty rosy cheeks. I had even brought her to our home to play one day during the summer.

"I'll tell you something, but you mustn't mention it to anyone!" Auntie Wang whispered in my ear.

"Of course!" I promised. I closed my door gently, then made her sit down by the desk while I sat on the edge of the bed.

"At ten o'clock last night," she continued in a whisper, leaning close to me so as not to be overheard, "after all the children were asleep, Lao Wang of the political section showed up, bringing with him Lao Shao of the broadcasting section and a tape recorder. The director of the kindergarten was with them. They told me to wake up Xiao Hong. She was sleeping so soundly I couldn't wake her, so I had to carry her into the dining room and wipe her face with a cold washcloth. Even after she opened her eyes she was still only half awake. Lao Shao turned on the tape recorder. Section Chief Wang closed the door, and then he and the director began to question Xiao Hong. First they asked her, 'What is your father's name? What is your mother's name?' Then 'Did anyone teach you to shout reactionary slogans?' Xiao Hong, whose eyes were still closed, kept shaking her head. After a while the director grew impatient and demanded, 'A little friend of yours said she heard you shouting a reactionary slogan . . .'" Now Auntie Wang's lips were almost touching my ear. "'Chairman Mao is a rotten egg.' Did you shout that?" Apparently the seriousness of the situation suddenly dawned on her, because she opened her eyes—you remember her eyes, as bright and shiny as lychee nut kernels—and she stared at Section Chief Wang, then at the director, shaking her head over and over.

"They took turns urging her to confess, to tell the truth and be Chairman Mao's good little girl. They said that if she would confess that would be the end of it. Finally the director told her the name of the friend who had reported her. That seemed to jog her memory, and she burst out crying. We had to comfort her for a long time before she quieted down. I thought that would be the end of the matter, but they began to question her again, 'Why did you shout that reactionary slogan? Where did you hear the slogan? Did your daddy say it? Did your mommy say it? Did your teacher say it?' Xiao Hong just kept shaking her head at every question. Aiya, Wen Laoshi, you don't know how frightened I was! I was in a cold sweat!"

At this point Auntie Wang straightened up; her eyes rolled back as though she were going to faint, and she was patting her chest with one hand.

"When I stole a glance at my watch I was shocked to find that it was already midnight. The poor child couldn't take any more and couldn't keep her eyes open. When they asked her again, 'Did you hear your mommy say it?' she just closed her eyes and nodded her head. They asked her, 'When did she say it? Where did you hear it?' but she couldn't answer anymore. Finally, after much fruitless questioning, they let me carry her back to bed. The moment she was in my arms she fell fast asleep. But I haven't been able to sleep a wink. It's been on my mind all day long."

No wonder she couldn't sleep; I was dumbstruck just hearing her talk about it.

"Did you say they taped everything?"

"Of course," Auntie Wang replied. "And it will be part of her record forever."

"Her record!" I hugged myself as I felt a sudden chill in my heart. "Heavens, she's just a child!"

"Yes, not yet four; a little younger than your Jingjing." Auntie Wang sighed.

I shook my head in disbelief. I felt, as Xiao Hong most probably had felt, that I must be dreaming. Shi Laoshi came from an approved background, I recalled, but his wife was from a landlord family and for that reason she tried harder in everything she did. Now their daughter had gotten into this terrible mess, and they were totally unaware of it. Poor Xiao Hong, only four years old, and already she had all of this recorded against her. The tape would be filed away, and if in the future she did anything out of line it would be brought out to prove that she had been a "reactionary since childhood."

No wonder Auntie Wang couldn't sleep. I was so upset myself that I tossed and turned all night. Xiao Hong's bright eyes and rosy cheeks kept appearing before me.

From then on, I asked Auntie Wang daily how things were going. First she had to make a written report, then the director of the kindergarten consulted with the school. Finally someone was sent to Xiao Hong's mother's home in Tianchang County to investigate her. Now I began to worry about the mother. And poor Shi Laoshi! All year long he traveled throughout the country investigating other people, never dreaming that his own wife would one day be the object of an investigation.

On Sunday evening, as An Nainai was washing the dishes in the kitchen and I was reading Jingjing a story from the children's book *Nabbing the Secret Agent by Strategy*, Auntie Wang came over. She looked around nervously, her small eyes bright with excitement and filled with mystery. Something unfortunate must have happened to Xiao Hong's mother. I gave Jingjing two pieces of candy and coaxed him into An Nainai's room to read a book, then gently closed the door behind him.

"How are things with Xiao Hong's mother?" I asked anxiously. I didn't even offer Auntie Wang a seat, but simply pointed to the chair at the desk. I propped up my belly and plopped down on the bed to await the news.

"Xiao Hong's mother?" Auntie Wang stared at me, shaking her head and waving her hands. "It's not Xiao Hong's mother. It's Jingjing!"

"Jingjing?" I repeated, completely at a loss.

"Aiya, what can I say?" She sat down in a chair, then, drawing it toward me, leaned over so close her chin nearly touched my belly as she whispered, "Dongdong told me that when he was playing with Jingjing this afternoon he heard Jingjing shout . . . he shouted a reactionary slogan!"

"A reactionary slogan? What slogan?" I still didn't understand.

"Aiya!" Unable to sit still any longer, she jumped up. Pressing close to my ear, she spat out the words, one by one, "He said: 'Chairman Mao is a rotten egg'!"

"What?!" I cried, springing to my feet.

"Shh! Not so loud!"

Auntie Wang caught hold of me and pressed me back onto the edge of the bed. I was completely numb, my mind a blank, as I muttered over and over, "Reactionary slogan . . . reactionary slogan . . ."

"The child's still young and can be straightened out. Speak to him. There's no need to spank him." Auntie Wang sat down beside me, trying to comfort me.

It was quite a while before I could pull myself together enough to ask, "Aside from Dongdong, who else heard him say it?"

"I don't know," she frowned, her head tilted in thought. "I think just the two of them were playing together."

I made up my mind to talk to Dongdong in order to get to the bottom of this. An Nainai was just then coming out of the kitchen, wiping her hands on her apron, as I started out of the room, dragging Auntie Wang after me. I was waddling with the weight of the child in me. "What's the matter?" An Nainai asked.

"We'll be right back!" I answered as we left for Auntie Wang's apartment. When Dongdong saw the look on my face he was badly frightened. His small eyes opened wide, he waved his hands, and he shook his head vigorously. "I didn't say anything! I didn't say anything! Jingjing said it!"

It was only after some questioning that I finally learned what had happened: That afternoon, as the two of them were playing in the garden, they had begun by calling anyone they could think of a "rotten egg." After shouting "Daddy's a rotten egg!" "Mommy's a rotten egg!" Jingjing had let slip the name of the one person he should never ever mention.

"I'm going to give him a good spanking!" Once my fear had subsided, anger surged through me. Holding my belly I stamped angrily on the cement walk.

"Spanking alone won't solve the problem, Wen Laoshi," Auntie Wang remonstrated. "You have to start from the beginning and teach him to love Chairman Mao. You must guide him into loving our leader."

"As if I haven't . . ." I choked up at the injustice of the insinuation, and tears began to flow.

Not love Chairman Mao? How could I begin to tell her! To start with, my husband had not wanted our child to be born in a foreign country, so we had rushed back to China so he could be born here. And even before he was born his school name had already been chosen: Weidong—Defend Mao Zedong. When he was but a few months old we were lifting him up to look at Chairman Mao's portrait so he'd recognize it as he grew up. He would laugh at the sight of his picture, and kick his legs and wave his arms. Before he could even say "Mama" he was crying out "Mao! Mao!" How could anyone say that he didn't love Chairman Mao? And we, his parents, did not lag behind. In

1969, when the entire country was fanatically promoting the Loyalty Campaign,* I went out for four hours every night after a full day's work to take my turn at embroidering the huge portrait of Chairman Mao. In response to the call from the rebel faction, every wall in our home, except in the kitchen and the toilet, was plastered with Chairman Mao's portraits, poetry, calligraphy, and the like. It was not until his wife, Jiang Qing, began to feel that all of this was too vulgar and gave the order to stop that we took them all down.

How could anyone say we did not love Chairman Mao? Why, in order to follow him we had abandoned our families and come to China, where we had neither friends nor relatives. Time and again my husband told Jingjing that Chairman Mao was the only family we had.

"Don't cry any more, Wen Laoshi." Auntie Wang tried to console me. "You're so big with child now that you mustn't get upset. As I said, Jingjing is still young and can be straightened out."

She talked as though Jingjing were already a hopeless case. All I wanted to do was cry my heart out. But I was afraid that the neighbors would hear me and that news of the incident would spread. So I took some deep breaths and silently wiped away the tears that kept rolling down my face. Suddenly the baby in my womb moved, and what should have filled me with

*The Loyalty Campaign (zhongzihua yundong) was supposedly initiated by the masses, but was highly endorsed by Lin Biao and his followers. Its objective was to worship and glorify Mao and promote his thought through daily life. At the beginning and end of each work day, everyone shouted "Long live Chairman Mao," recited his teachings, sang songs of praise, and danced before his picture. Every school and factory had a Loyalty Room in which were displayed many types of handicrafts, all with one subject—Mao; and in every household the walls were to be covered with objects related to him.

mystery and great happiness was only a throbbing pain. Forgetting my tears, I pressed both hands against my belly.

"Dongdong," Auntie Wang admonished her son, "you're not to tell anyone about Jingjing! If you do I'll give you a spanking, and Jingjing won't play with you anymore!"

Dongdong stared at his mother with tiny eyes that resembled hers. He nodded his little head repeatedly like a grave old man.

I went home filled with anger. Nainai had just finished bathing Jingjing and was dressing him as I rushed into the room.

"What's the matter, Wen Laoshi?"

I began questioning Jingjing without even answering her. He raised his plump little face, mouth open, eyes blinking as he pulled at his wet hair; the incident was obviously not preying on his mind.

"Dongdong said you shouted 'Chairman Mao . . .'" At this point I hesitated and from force of habit looked around before continuing in a lowered voice, "'is a rotten egg!' Did you say that?"

"May I hope to die!" An Nainai gasped as she stamped her foot out of fright.

At this he seemed to remember. His face tightened and he stared at me with fearful eyes.

"Did you or did you not say that?" I demanded again.

"Yes, I did." His voice was as soft as a mosquito's.

"Why?" I screamed angrily.

His face was now devoid of expression. His mouth hung open foolishly and his eyes were as dull as those of a dead fish. Even in my anger I felt sorry for him, but my heart was filled with foreboding. So many parents had said to me, "A child may steal or rob, but he must never ever commit a political error."

Armed with this thought, I leaned over and slapped him hard on each cheek. This took him completely by surprise; he covered his face and burst into tears.

"Ah, don't be so hard on the child!" the frightened old woman said as she pulled him away from me. Jingjing cried louder than ever, holding his tear-streaked cheeks with his hands. "Don't you ever say that again!" An Nainai scolded, with a set face. "Only counterrevolutionaries say such things. If you say it again I'll smack your mouth! See what you've done to your mother! Now, promise you'll never say it again."

"Won't . . . say it . . . ," he managed to gasp between sobs.

"Come, let's wash your face again." An Nainai dragged him off to the kitchen before I could say another word.

What'll I do? I kept asking myself. Completely exhausted, I walked slowly to my room. I closed the door, leaned against the wall, and closed my eyes tightly, wishing I could shut out everything and not have to worry about a thing. The turmoil in my mind was like the rising and falling waves of a raging sea futilely searching for the land. I wasn't even sure whether I was anxious for Jingjing or for myself. I had the sudden urge to write my husband, but was afraid that if the letter were censored it could be used as damaging evidence. I decided it was better to wait until he came home; that would also save him a few days of anxiety. Such anxiety would, of course, pass in time, but what concerned me most was that he might be disappointed in his son. That would be a tremendous emotional blow for him. After traveling thousands of miles to return to China, he had met with so much personal frustration. His only hope was that his son, born and raised under the red flag, would grow up as an accepted member of the eight hundred million people, living a peaceful life without the burden of any previous ideology. And now Jingjing was but four years old, and this humble hope was already in danger of being dashed. How could my husband bear such a blow?

After much thought, I decided not to tell him about the incident—not even after he came home. But how was I to stop others from bringing it up? I was sure I could ask An Nainai not to say anything, and I could hint at it to Auntie Wang. Since she and my husband were from the same province, and since the Cantonese are well known for their loyalty, I was confident that she would not report the matter to the school authorities. But I wasn't so sure of her husband. He was a colleague of mine, a man with a reputation for being very progressive. Besides, he had close ties to Party members and high officials. He had always kept me at a polite distance, even though his wife and I were close friends, most probably because I had been poisoned by an "American imperialist" education. I decided that from then on I must be extra careful not to offend him. Neither could I afford to offend Auntie Wang or, for that matter, even Dongdong.

At the thought that I, a grown woman, had to be on guard against a seven-year-old child, my cheeks flushed. This was all Jingjing's doing! I was extremely angry as I walked away from the wall toward the desk. I closed my ears to the whimpering coming from the next room. The baby inside me moved again; I felt as though an electric current were running through my whole body. Hugging myself tightly, I quickly sat down.

On the desk was a huge pile of books, composed exclusively of the sayings, poems, and essays of Mao Zedong. There were various editions: hard-covered ones, pocket books, and every other kind that was available. I sighed as I raised my head to look at the portrait of Chairman Mao hanging on the wall in front of me. He seemed to be smiling slightly, as if unmoved by what had just taken place. His cold, aloof look gave me a momentary fright.

At that moment the baby moved again. First I felt numb, then there was a dull pain. I held myself tightly, silently assuring my unborn child: Don't worry, when you come into the world I'll find an excuse to take that portrait off the wall.

Thus, I sat in my room, thinking, planning, and worrying deep into the night before turning out the light and going to bed.

At daybreak An Nainai got up to prepare breakfast. I rose at six o'clock since I had to go to the market. I had hardly slept at all and I looked haggard; my eyes were swollen and my mouth was dry. I felt top-heavy and not too steady on my feet, and I could see that the old woman was concerned.

"You didn't sleep well," she said, "so go back to bed and I'll do the shopping."

I shook my head, muttering without even really knowing what I was saying, "His father will be coming home soon."

"Now don't you go telling him about it!" she advised me firmly, sensing what was on my mind. "I don't think you should worry so much. What can they do to such a small child for saying something wrong, kill him? In our Huaian County the farmers always use Chairman Mao's name when they swear or take a pledge. It's worse when they start cursing! Many of them have been poor peasants for three generations, and nobody ever did anything to them!"

An Nainai's simple honesty comforted me, but there was no way I could make her understand the great difference in the political treatment of peasants and intellectuals.

When Jingjing got up he was smiling just as usual, even

though his eyes were slightly swollen. He'd already forgotten all about the trouble he'd caused.

"Mommy, is today my birthday?" he asked as he picked up his bowl of rice porridge.

I ignored him, my face taut. I was angry, yet amused. After all, a child is still a child. Looking at his plump little face, so innocent, I thought of his classmate Xiao Hong, and in my mind's eye I could see a child being questioned late into the night. Only this time it was Jingjing. The thought killed my appetite, and I couldn't taste what I was eating. An Nainai, trying to tempt me to eat, opened a bottle of Hangzhou fermented bean curd that someone had given her. Thanks to her, I managed to force down my bowl of rice porridge, although I didn't do justice to the famous delicacy she had placed before me.

At a quarter to eight I led Jingjing out the door, just as the Zhuos, who lived next door to us, were coming out of their apartment. Mr. Zhuo, meticulously dressed in his Mao jacket, stepped briskly along with his head held high, while thin, tiny Mrs. Zhuo followed behind him. The moment she saw me she smiled.

"Good morning, Wen Laoshi."

"Good morning!" I answered hastily, carefully scrutinizing their faces. Mr. Zhuo nodded at me with a faint smile, then lifted his head again and walked steadily on. Mrs. Zhuo stopped to pat Jingjing on the head before hurrying after her husband. I purposely slowed down, and in a little while the Zhuos' two sons came out. They were already in middle school and proudly wore Red Guard bands on their arms. They stopped and, with smiling faces, called out "Jingjing" before hurrying on. These two Red Guards didn't seem to have behaved any differently than usual, so I figured they couldn't know about Jingjing. I was greatly relieved, but I'd also have to be careful of the Zhuo family.

It was no accident that the school authorities had placed us in this dormitory. There were three families in our wing: our door was opposite the Wangs', and the Zhuos lived between us. Mr. Wang came from a scholarly family in Nanjing, where his father had been a professor. But because his grandfather had been an official in the Nationalist government, he had always been ultra-radical in order to prove his loyalty to the Party. People said that at the beginning of the Red Guard movement, when the posters proclaimed that it was forbidden to use household help, he immediately fired Dongdong's nainai. Dongdong had weighed less than three catties at birth, and the old woman had taken care of him from the time he was taken out of the incubator at the hospital. The separation was a cruel one. Four years is a long time, and they had grown very close to one another. Nainai and Dongdong, and even Auntie Wang, broke down and cried. Mr. Wang alone, frowning silently, remained unmoved.

His was the first family in our compound to respond to the call of the Red Guards, so to show their appreciation the Guards tore down the poster pasted on his door, to the accompaniment of drums and gongs. Later, as the number of unemployed women grew, they petitioned Premier Zhou to intervene, and shortly thereafter a notice was quietly circulated that permission to hire household help could be given under certain circumstances. By then Mr. Wang had joined the May Seventh movement and was in the labor reform program in northern Jiangsu. Since Auntie Wang often had to work the night shift, she wanted to have the old woman back, but Mr. Wang was adamant. On nights when the temperature fell below zero, poor Auntie Wang had to wrap Dongdong up in so many quilts he looked like a football and carry him on her back. Sometimes when it was snowing I would take pity on the child and insist on keeping him, letting him sleep with Jingjing. It was because of this episode that I stood in awe and fear of Mr. Wang.

Mr. and Mrs. Zhuo were both important Party members. Since they were always being sent out to attend meetings or to investigate questionable colleagues, they were never able to find the time to go work on the farm. Maybe that was the reason they were both so enthusiastic over the greatness of the farm labor program, loudly praising Chairman Mao's May Seventh Directive and declaring how this path should be followed to the end. That was particularly true of Mr. Zhuo, who was an expert on all the political phrases and terms and spouted them fluently. Behind his back people called him the "super-leftist," but no one dared ask him to his face when he would personally follow the path of the May Seventh Directive. The Zhuos' sons surpassed even their parents in their zeal. At the beginning of the Cultural Revolution, when the boys were only elementary school students, they were already very proficient in organizing the other children to "search and confiscate" among the families in our dormitory. They were fierce and unrelenting, and everyone in the compound—young and old—was wary of them.

"Remember, Jingjing," I warned him, "you're not to go and play at Auntie Zhuo's place anymore." But I knew that the safest way would be to try to keep him at home.

On the morning of September eleventh, I woke up with great excitement; my husband would be arriving that noon. Now that what I'd looked forward to for such a long time was coming true, I felt apprehensive. My pounding heart grew heavy, weighing me down.

Just as I finished washing up, An Nainai came in with a smile to show me what she'd bought. She'd gotten up at four o'clock to buy fresh vegetables and fish at the Dragon Way open market. The sight of her purchases and her smiling face made me happy, but also somewhat ashamed. I had lived in China several years, but I still hadn't acquired the habit of giving up sleep for the sake of satisfying my appetite.

As I was about to leave for work, taking Jingjing along as usual, An Nainai said, "His daddy's coming home today, so why are you sending him to kindergarten?"

"Mommy, I don't want to go!" Jingjing protested.

"I think you'd better go," I said after thinking it over. "Nainai can work better then."

He was very disappointed, but just then the Wangs' door opened and Dongdong came out, satchel in hand, behind his mother. The moment the two children saw each other they began talking, and Jingjing's protest was quickly forgotten. Then the members of the Zhuo family emerged from their door, and after a flurry of greetings, we all went our separate ways.

It was a beautiful sunny day; everything was bright and clear. The path to the kindergarten was lined with French parasol trees, and the sunlight filtering through the leaves cast speckled shadows on the cobbled path, flitting and dancing in the breeze. Even as I stepped on the dappled shadows my mind was busily trying to analyze the facial expressions of the neighbors from whom we had just parted: The "super-leftist" had held his head high in his usual unapproachable manner. Had his wife stopped to pat Jingjing's head? The two Zhuo boys had hurried away after calling out, "Auntie Wen." Had they been in a hurry to go to school or were they trying to avoid me? And Auntie Wang had called out only a brief good morning to me, then hurried off to chat with Mrs. Zhuo about the weather. Seeing her so friendly with this Party member, I wondered if she would tell her about Jingjing.

As I walked and wondered my head began to ache. Jingjing was skipping and running ahead of me. As I followed him my forehead dripped with perspiration, and my stomach tightened spasmodically. I wiped my forehead with one hand and held my belly with the other, panting heavily. When I finally reached the kindergarten, the other children were already there, and I saw Xiao Hong sitting on the floor playing with some wooden blocks. She was wearing a pink smock on which her mother had embroidered the words "Love Labor." Suddenly she raised her head and called out, "Hi, Jingjing's mommy." I managed to smile at her before I turned away, for my eyes were filling with tears.

When I came home at noon I was surprised to find Jingjing sitting on his father's lap with his face wreathed in smiles.

"What's the matter with you? You look terrible!" my husband cried. He put Jingjing down, hurried over to hold me, and made me sit down on the edge of the bed.

"Nothing," I said. "I just walked too fast."

Jingjing stood on a chair and began to leaf through the pile of children's books on the table, exclaiming, "Look, Mommy! Daddy brought me all these books!"

I could tell at a glance that they were the usual comic books about catching special agents. I said nothing, although I really didn't like these children's books, for they filled the children's minds with the concept of spies and special agents. In Jingjing's mind there were only two kinds of people in the world: good ones and spies. It was as if China had become a nation of spies.

It had been a long time since my husband and I had seen one another, and there was so very much to say. But now we just looked at one another, not knowing where to begin. His hair was clipped short, his face was deeply tanned, and he looked healthy and strong. His patched blue cloth shirt and trousers had turned gray from many washings and were covered with new patches. He didn't look any different from the laborers in the commune on the outskirts of Nanjing.

An Nainai was cooking lunch in the kitchen, and the house filled with the fragrance of fish cooked in wine. My husband smiled faintly and looked at my large belly, but all he said was, "The food smells good!"

"Lunch is ready!" An Nainai called. "Go wash your hands, Jingjing."

Jingjing reluctantly left his books, climbed off his chair, and went into the kitchen.

"You must be careful when you buy children's books," I quickly told my husband. "Don't buy any that have too many pictures of Chairman Mao."

"Don't worry," he answered with an understanding smile. "My colleagues have already warned me that it's best not to buy comic books like those about the heroes Lei Feng and Wang Jie, as there are pictures of Chairman Mao on almost every other page. Children have caused a lot of trouble by spoiling the Chairman's picture when they color the books."

He leaned closer to me, lowering his voice to a whisper. "My colleagues remove the pages with Chairman Mao's pictures on them before they give the books to their children. I've done the same thing. Just don't say anything about it. We've got to be very careful with Jingjing. He's at a difficult age, understanding the words we say, but not fully comprehending their meaning. Don't let him draw on the ground, and don't give him any chalk or pencils. If he should get into trouble, with our background we couldn't clear ourselves even if we jumped into the sea to wash our sins away. And now with the old woman living with us, we must be extra careful. These days one must always be on guard."

"Yes, yes," I hastily agreed, avoiding his eyes as I felt another dull pain.

During lunch both my husband and An Nainai kept heaping fish and vegetables into Jingjing's bowl.

"Jing, have you been a good boy at home?" his father asked him. "Have you done anything naughty?"

"No!" Jingjing declared unhesitatingly, busily stuffing fish into his mouth.

An Nainai looked at him, then went on eating without saying a word.

My husband kept urging me to eat more fish. "A pregnant woman must eat fish. It contains a lot of calcium and phosphorous."

I felt a bit guilty when I looked at his bright, cheerful face, filled with the joy of being home again. As I listened to him tell how he had learned to cut hair and patch clothes I pulled myself together and finished my lunch.

On my way back to work in the afternoon I met Dongdong's father. He was pushing his bicycle along with one hand and balancing a large covered food tray with the other. One look and I knew that he had bought roast duck from the famous restaurant Da Sanyuan. He nodded politely as I greeted him, his white teeth showing up against his dark face.

After dinner that evening, while my husband was waiting for his bath water to heat, Jingjing and I took our stools out into the garden as usual to sit for a while. In Nanjing, as soon as September arrives the mornings and evenings grow cool, and it is pleasant to sit outside after dinner. During the summer many of the families even move out into the garden to eat their dinners. Every day at twilight our compound was crowded with tables and chairs, as the teachers and their entire families sat around in T-shirts and shorts, a fan in one hand and a pair of chopsticks in the other. The evenings would ring with their laughter and spirited conversation.

That night we sat in our usual spot under the Wangs' kitchen window. Auntie Wang, who always came home from work late, was just then beginning to cook dinner. The smell of vegetables and oyster sauce wafted out through the window. As she walked around the kitchen she was humming a tune that was unfamiliar to me—this was unprecedented; I had always thought that she knew only revolutionary songs. I could see only the upper half of her body; she was wearing a bright red short-sleeved blouse, her hair was newly trimmed, and she smiled as she worked. She was a typical southern woman, always dressed in up-to-date clothes, but this was the first time I'd seen her in such bright colors. Seeing her so happily occupied, I hadn't the heart to greet her. Many of the teachers who had just returned from work were outside in the compound busily greeting each other. It seemed noisier than a special holiday.

At about nine-thirty, when Jingjing and An Nainai were in

bed and my husband and I were preparing to retire, there suddenly came the sound of a child crying. I recognized Dongdong's voice and, startled, began to put on the blouse I'd just taken off.

"Don't meddle in other people's affairs," my husband said.

"I'll just take a look," I answered as I hurried to open our door. I saw that Mrs. Zhuo had already poked her head out her door to listen.

"What's going on?" I asked her. "Why is Dongdong crying so hard?"

"I don't know," she answered, as she opened her door a little wider.

Dongdong's father had been talking in a loud voice, and suddenly, as though someone had pulled the plug on the radio, there was no more sound. Even Dongdong's crying trailed off and become a soft sobbing. Mrs. Zhuo and I listened for a while but we could hear nothing more, so we closed our doors.

"What was it?" my husband asked as I came back to bed.

"Nothing," I answered. "Dongdong was crying."

And yet I was worried. We'd been neighbors for several years and I'd seldom heard Dongdong cry. The Wangs loved their son dearly and never raised their voices when talking to him. I worried that it might have something to do with Jingjing, and I didn't sleep well that night. I woke constantly, the child within me so heavy I had a hard time breathing.

The next day was Sunday. I purposely left our door open, hoping that Dongdong would come over to play, but I neither saw nor heard anyone from the Wang family. I urged my husband to take Jingjing to the Ming Tombs and the Sun Yat-sen Mausoleum, but he said that since it was Sunday it would be too crowded; he'd take the boy on the following day, which was his birthday. Meanwhile, it had been a long time since he'd gone downtown, so right after an early lunch he took Jingjing and went off light-heartedly.

In the afternoon the coal man delivered our ration of a hundred coal bricks, which he piled up in front of the door. An Nainai would not let me help as she carried them four at a time into the kitchen and stacked them under the sink. Since I couldn't help her, I began to sweep up the coal dust. The Wangs' door was slightly ajar, and Dongdong peeped out at me.

"Dongdong, where's your mother?" I asked as I swept.

"Taking a nap," he whispered, opening the door a little wider to stick out his head.

"Why were you crying last night?" I asked in a whisper.

He gazed at me silently, his eyes blinking.

"Your father didn't scold you, did he?"

He hesitated, then said slowly, "He spanked me." He blinked, as though he were still feeling the hurt.

"Really!" I cried out in surprise, dropping the broom and knocking over a coal brick, which shattered into pieces.

"See what you've done!" An Nainai came rushing over, upset over the waste. She snatched the broom away from me and did the sweeping herself.

"Why did your father spank you?" I walked over to him. Pressing close to the door, I whispered, "Did you do something bad?"

"I said a reactionary slogan," he admitted ingenuously.

"What?" I gasped. "It was *you* who said it? Now exactly who said it, you or Jingjing?"

He nodded, then shook his head.

"I won't say it again. Daddy told me not to tell anyone . . ."

"Dongdong!" Mr. Wang suddenly called from inside, frightening the boy. Dongdong pulled his head back in and slammed the door.

"What's happened?" An Nainai had heard only part of the conversation. She straightened up, forgetting her sweeping, and stared at me inquisitively. "Who said it?"

"Maybe it wasn't Jingjing after all." I began to feel a glimmer of hope. Just then, since the door had been slammed hard against my belly, I felt a stab of pain.

"What's the matter?" the old woman asked as she saw me clutch my belly with both hands.

"It's nothing," I answered reassuringly. Then I felt my womb constricting into a tight ball and I was frightened. "I'll go lie down for a while."

But how could I rest? I paced up and down in the room, holding my belly as I anxiously waited for my husband and son to return. I couldn't be sure how much time had passed before I heard Jingjing's voice calling out, "Mommy!" When An Nainai hurried out to open the door, he came rushing in, a box in his hand. "Mommy, new shoes! Daddy's going to take me to the Mausoleum tomorrow on my birthday!"

I rushed over and grabbed him. "Come with me," I cried, dragging him into the bedroom. My husband immediately followed us inside, asking, "What's the matter?"

I pulled Jingjing over to the desk and, with a stern look, pointed to Chairman Mao's portrait, demanding in a low voice, "Jingjing, I want you to tell me the truth. Dongdong said that he was the one who said the reactionary slogan. Now did he or didn't he?"

The moment he heard the words "reactionary slogan" and looked at Chairman Mao's portrait his face froze.

"Reactionary slogan? What reactionary slogan?" My husband grew tense and agitated as he grasped Jingjing's shoulders tightly.

"I didn't say it!" Jingjing shook his head repeatedly as he gazed fearfully at his father. "I didn't say it. It was Dongdong . . ."

"Ah!" I let out a sigh of relief. I felt as though a weight had been lifted, and my heart soared.

"What did he say? Tell me quickly!" His father frantically shook him by the shoulders. "What did he say? Where did he say it?"

"In the yard," Jingjing stammered, pointing to the window. "Dongdong dared me . . . to say Chairman Mao . . . a rotten egg. But I wouldn't say it. It was Dongdong who said it!"

"When was this? Answer me this minute!" I demanded impatiently.

"I think it must have been yesterday afternoon," An Nainai interrupted. She had followed us unnoticed into the room. "They were playing in the yard for a while."

"Yesterday?" Stunned and disappointed, I felt as if I'd fallen from a cloud.

"What? Children saying reactionary words like that!" My husband's face was dark with anger as he shook the child fiercely. Jingjing was so frightened he burst into tears.

"Stop crying!" my husband shouted. "How about it? Did you say it or didn't you? Answer me right this minute!"

Jingjing cried even louder. I began to feel faint. An Nainai caught hold of me, crying out, "Oh, oh, look at her face!" I was taken to the hospital that very day and after a whole night's ordeal I gave birth, a couple of weeks early, to our second child.

My colleagues often remark with envy, "Wen Laoshi, your two sons have the same birthday." I invariably answer with a smile, "Thanks to Chairman Mao."

And truly I did have Chairman Mao to thank, for from then on Auntie Wang became my close friend, and even her husband nodded and smiled whenever he saw me.

Night
Duty

Liu Xiangdong strode into the dining hall of the collective farm, a large bowl tucked under his arm and a pair of chopsticks in his hand. The place was already packed, with long lines in front of each food-stall window, even the one in the far corner where soup was usually sold. There was good reason why the hall was more crowded than usual that night: the teachers who had just arrived that afternoon had come in for dinner after being assigned their beds, and those who were returning to Nanjing the next morning lined up early to enjoy their last meal at the farm. Since there was no more room at the tables, most of the people were eating their food standing up. Xiangdong took his place at the end of one of the lines and dug into his pocket for his rice and vegetable coupons as he studied the menu pasted on the wall.

The day's menu, written with black ink on a piece of bright red paper, had caught his eye at once. To express their welcome to the newcomers and their farewell to those who were leaving, the kitchen staff had prepared several special dishes: a meatball called lion's head, sweet-and-sour pork, and the saltwater duck of which Nanjing people are so proud. The menu stimulated his appetite, and as he watched the people around him devouring their food, his stomach began to growl. His appetite had greatly increased since his return to China the year before. He was eating twice as much and having no more stomach trouble; in America he had always been concerned that he might have ulcers. The thought struck him that a man's stomach really adapts in quick order.

> Soldiers of the revolution, each must remember
> To observe the three regulations and eight points:
> First, obedience in every action . . .

The farm's broadcasting had begun. Xiangdong did not need a watch to know that it was five-thirty. Every morning the loudspeakers blared out "The East Is Red" to rouse everyone out of bed; then there were revolutionary songs for relaxation during lunchtime and work breaks; and finally "The East Is Red" sent everyone off to bed again. Life was thus regulated, never changing, making a watch entirely superfluous. During his first days in Nanjing, before he'd grown accustomed to the shrill loudspeakers, Xiangdong had felt that they violated his personal freedom, interfered with his train of thought, and virtually forced him into conforming. He'd even toyed with the idea of mentioning these objections to the comrade leader as a suggestion for improvement. But he soon discovered that the broadcasting was an integral part of daily life in New China, so he forced himself to accept it, eventually learning to take it in stride. Once, during rice planting season, when the work was heavy and especially tiring, he'd actually fallen asleep before the broadcast ended.

"Hurry! Hurry! We're all out of saltwater duck! Cabbage is three fen a plate."

This shout greeted him as he reached the window. Peering in through the small opening, Xiangdong could see that all the good food had indeed been given out, so he had to be satisfied with two small dishes of sliced meat with greens and some rice. Holding his bowl carefully, he looked around for a place by a window, where it would not be so crowded, to stand and eat.

"Liu Xiangdong! Come join us!" Lao He, from Xiangdong's dormitory, was signaling with his chopsticks. Lao He and three or four colleagues from Xiangdong's department had a table to themselves and were already eating heartily. They squeezed over to let him have a corner of one of the benches.

"You're late. The duck is already sold out," said Lao He.

"It doesn't matter," Xiangdong said with an indifferent shrug. Being a "grasslander," a Taiwanese peasant, he still could not appreciate saltwater duck and found the plain cooked duck of his native Taiwan much tastier. From the piles of bones at both ends of the table, he could see that the others had all eaten duck.

"Xiao Liu, will you be getting into the classroom when you return?" a comrade sitting opposite him asked, as he spit out a bone and noisily scraped his bowl clean.

"Assisting in first-year college math," Lao He answered for him, enviously.

Xiangdong muttered an acknowledgment and made no further comment as he pretended to be engrossed in his food. The policy of rotating labor not only disrupted teaching schedules but also caused many teachers to lose their jobs upon their return from a period of labor. Naturally the teachers were envious of anyone who had classes to go back to. Xiangdong himself was eager to get back to the classroom, but since the universities had just started taking in students again, there were only first-year classes, so he would have to wait until the third year before it was decided whether he would be able to teach his specialty. Rather than remain idle for two years, he had urgently requested that he be placed on the frontlines of teaching. His group leader responded by putting him down for a so-called assistantship, which was to begin as soon as Xiangdong returned from his period of labor. In reality the job was to assist the math teacher by helping the students with their lessons during class and in the dormitories.

Xiangdong's earnest determination to dedicate his energies to the socialist motherland enabled him to ignore being laughed at for using his talents at such a low level. He had even brought along a number of reference books so he could prepare himself while he was still at the farm. As luck would have it, there was a young teacher in the same labor group who had just come from assisting in a math course. Xiangdong had immediately asked his help and advice. At first the young man was aghast at the large pile of books; then he burst out laughing. At the first opportunity he took Xiangdong aside and informed him that first-year mathematics began with decimal points and addition, and that even when the students graduated, they would not be up to taking calculus, let alone more sophisticated subjects.

"If you can make them understand that zero point one added to zero point one equals zero point two, and that one-half added to one-half does not equal one-fourth, you'll have done your job."

This revelation greatly disappointed Xiangdong. He carefully tied up his books, placed them under his straw mattress, and never again mentioned his assistantship. He knew that he could not blame his disappointment on the students—they were assigned to the university to study mathematics, and it was no fault of theirs. What was it then? Why was he so upset and disheartened? He wasn't able to find the answer, and his distress became a lead weight on his heart.

"Comrades, attention!" The revolutionary songs were suddenly broken off for a report. "Tonight at seven o'clock sharp all comrades will please come to the dining hall for a meeting to evaluate the achievements of these three months of labor. We also want to welcome the new group of teachers who have joined us in following Chairman Mao's May Seventh Directive. After the commune Party Committee makes its report, each study group representative will report what his group has learned from this period of labor. There will be group discussions after the general meeting ends. Please be on time."

Everyone had known about this meeting for some time, so the announcement aroused no excitement.

"It's the last night, so let's hope the meeting won't last too late." So saying, Lao He picked up his bowl and was the first to leave.

"What I've learned is exactly the same as last time, so I'll finish what I have to say in two minutes," a colleague sitting next to Xiangdong said lightly. He had finished eating, his white porcelain bowl already scraped clean. Suddenly he turned to Xiangdong. "This is the first time you've followed the May Seventh Directive. You must have acquired many deep impressions, so you can give a long speech tonight."

At the word "speech" Xiangdong reddened slightly, and said hurriedly, "I'll wait until I get back to Nanjing to talk. Since I'm on duty tonight, the group leader has given me permission to miss the meeting."

"You really should attend," another colleague said considerately, "since you'll be going back to Nanjing tomorrow. If you go on duty tonight you won't be able to catch up on your sleep. It's not worth it."

"It doesn't matter; the loss of a night's sleep won't bother me."

In fact, it was just such self-serving motivation on everyone else's part that had given Xiangdong the opportunity to take the watch that night. Having attended the same kind of meeting three months before, he had deliberately sought a way to absent himself from this one. At the earlier meeting he had listened to the previous group of teachers get up and expound emotionally on the effects of their having joined in the reeducation process under the poor and lower-middle peasants in northern Jiangsu province. They had waxed enthusiastic about how their views of life had changed and how their convictions had completely turned around. For them it had been a rebirth. Some teachers had even wept profusely, and he himself had been so moved by what he heard that he'd clenched his hands into tight fists until his palms were wet with perspiration.

The blink of an eye, and three months had passed. Now he dreaded the thought of this meeting, for he knew that when the time came he could not be like the others—emotional, eloquent, singing praises, just like players in a splendid drama.

But his colleagues intended no sarcasm. Xiangdong was aware of his own speech-making talent. A few years earlier in the United States, during the Diaoyutai movement,* he and several like-minded friends had talked all the way from Berkeley to Chicago. From platforms, car tops, or any place where he

---

*A group of eight small islands on the oil-rich continental shelf near Taiwan. In 1971, overseas Chinese launched a campaign to protect China's sovereignty over the islands after Japan proclaimed ownership.

could stand, he had spoken for hours on end. What supported him then was not only heartfelt patriotism but also a beautiful ideal, for which he stayed up nights to study the works of Lenin and Mao Zedong, always taking copious notes. Fearful of being investigated by the FBI, he did not dare to close his eyes at night unless his papers were safely under his pillow.

He reflected upon those enormously exciting days. By comparison, life after the return to his own country had been quiet and uneventful. Except for these three months of personal involvement in farm labor, the rest of his time had been entirely devoted to the Anti–Lin Biao campaign and study sessions. He had spent six whole months studying a thin volume, *The State and Revolution*, poring over each word and sentence, nearly memorizing the entire book. Initially he had joined the discussions, especially after discovering that a great many teachers hadn't the slightest idea of the inevitability of "the withering away of the state mechanism" and the future of Communism. He had quoted all sorts of theories and sayings to prove not only the possibility but the inevitability of this future society. The more he talked, the more intoxicated he became with the ideal of a utopian world. Once he even lost track of how long he'd been talking, only to discover that one of his colleagues was fast asleep. The discussion leader, yawning, had forced a smile when his eyes met Xiangdong's. Maybe this was what had earned him the reputation of "speechmaker."

What pained him, however, was not his nickname, but the truth about these higher-level intellectuals. Little by little, it dawned on him that they were given to discussing for the sake of discussion alone; that what they said was not what was actually in their hearts; and, furthermore, that they often used questions in order to pour out their own frustrations. This last realization hurt him the most, and he could not help but begin to doubt: Here in the acknowledged center of the world's revolution, just how many people truly believed in the theories of Marx and Lenin and the thought of Mao Zedong? Like so many other questions, this one had no answer. So as his reputation as a "speechmaker" spread, he actually grew more reticent.

"Take your time. Eat slowly."

One by one his colleagues left the table, and soon Xiangdong found himself alone. Only a few people were scattered around the dining hall, and the stillness was broken only by the revolutionary songs blaring from the loudspeaker. Someone sat down on the bench opposite him. It was the young peasant hired by the farm to weave baskets. With a grin at Xiangdong, the young man used his aluminum lunch box to push away the bones on the table and clear a space for himself. All he had were three large *mantou*, which he took out of his lunch box, and a dish of greens. Xiangdong glanced again at the bones strewn all over the table and was too embarrassed to look back at the man opposite him, who was by then devouring one of the steamed buns.

"Are you going back to Nanjing tomorrow?" the young man asked.

"Yes. How about you? Will you be going home to Huaian soon?"

The peasant stuffed in two large mouthfuls of greens with his chopsticks before answering. "Not certain yet. After I finish the baskets on your farm, if there's no more work around here, then I guess I'll go back." With that, he picked up the second *mantou*. His cheeks were all puffed out, one higher than the other. His large, round face was deeply tanned, and he stared out from under heavy black eyebrows at the *mantou* in front of his nose.

Xiangdong had passed the time of day with the man before and knew that he was called Weidong—Defend Mao Zedong—a popular name adopted after the Cultural Revolution, as was Xiangdong—Toward Mao Zedong—for that matter. Xiangdong also knew that the man was from a poor peasant family. He looked to be in his early twenties, and since he hardly ever talked or paid any attention to others, he was not well liked. The farm treasurer often complained behind his back that he was a lazy worker. It all stemmed from the fact that the contract between the farm and his commune was based on an hourly wage, not on piecework. And so he would often take his own sweet time, spending two or three days to complete one basket. Once the treasurer—who was an old Party member—simply couldn't take it any longer and tried to negotiate a new contract, based on piecework. He met with a flat refusal: "Contract labor? That's Liu Shaoqi's revisionist line. Wasn't the Cultural Revolution supposed to do away with that line of thought? Chairman Mao tells us always to trust in the people, to rely on the poor and lower-middle peasants." Everything the peasant said was strictly in accordance with Mao's teachings, and the treasurer, his face and ears a bright red, could find nothing more to say. Although Xiangdong had learned this secondhand, it made him regard the man differently.

"You've been away for quite some time. Aren't you homesick?" Xiangdong asked as he scraped away at his rice bowl.

The man grunted and raised his heavy eyebrows. It was not until he had swallowed the food in his mouth that he answered, coldly, "Going back will only mean more labor—land labor."

Xiangdong nodded. He scraped the remaining kernels of rice into his mouth and stood up to go. As he was about to lift his right leg over the bench he heard a dry laugh.

"Your kind of labor, huh!"

Xiangdong was so stunned by this comment that his face

turned red. But the man seemed to be talking to himself, muttering softly as he stared at the last remaining *mantou*, a corner of his mouth lifted in a sneer. Picking up his bowl, Xiangdong pushed aside the bench and walked away in silence.

May nights in northern Jiangsu are cool and mild. A half moon hung on the edge of a sky with just a sprinkling of stars, and the sparsely scattered lights of the farmhouses made the sky seem especially vast and lofty. The plains spread out endlessly, far and wide. Xiangdong was strolling alone, holding his arms behind his back. The water in the ditches on either side of the road trickled into the rice fields, and in the boundless quiet the sound was discordant yet familiar. Everything about this night served to arouse in him memories of his homeland. At night in his old hometown of Hualien it would be the time for insects to buzz and ocean breezes to blow. There the mountains would be shadowy and obscure, the moon would seem low enough to touch with your hand. There was no similarity to these vast and all-encompassing flat plains, which made him feel infinitely small, to the point of helplessness. In truth, he could not say when this feeling of helplessness had set in, but it was certainly intensifying as the days passed. He could not help being surprised that within a year of his return to the fatherland his state of mind should have undergone such a great change. He seemed to be getting old before his time. How long was it since he and some close friends, all determined idealists, had stood facing the icy cliffs of the Grand Tetons and recited Chairman Mao's poem "Snow"? Loudly and clearly they had sung the words, "For men of talent the time is now."

Where had this proud, brave spirit disappeared to? Back then he had given up his doctoral thesis and would gladly have forfeited his life in defense of the sacred territory of Diaoyutai.

But what had happened to Diaoyutai since then? He had once posed this question to a colleague at the university. The man had scratched his head for a moment before replying. "Diaoyutai? Isn't that located south of Beijing? I think that's the place where they entertain the higher-echelon officials and visiting dignitaries." Xiangdong never mentioned it again.

At times he wondered if he might be guilty of being an immature leftist who lacked dispassion, one whose strong patriotic emotions had deteriorated into regret and disillusionment. When he returned in 1973 he had been filled with an intense fighting spirit. But during his first two weeks in Beijing, in the midst of his sightseeing, he'd discovered that nothing at all was known about the situation in Taiwan. Whenever Taiwan was mentioned, the middle-echelon cadremen would quote outdated information and statistics. Then they would say that the Taiwanese eked out their living by selling their children or would predict that as soon as the fatherland decided to "liberate" Taiwan, all the people would rise and welcome the conquerors with food and drink.

Xiangdong was so shocked that he stayed up all night writing a long memorandum, which he sent to the State Council the day before he left Beijing. He also called on the Taiwan Democratic Self-Government League, only to discover that their knowledge and way of thinking were separated from his by at least a generation. They were not only ignorant of the average per-capita income of an ordinary Taiwanese laborer but also unaware of the actual significance of "self-government." He was so upset and angry that he stalked out without even sipping a mouthful of tea. Thinking back now, he sorely regretted his actions.

His memorandum was like a stone cast into the ocean. Still,

in the editorial for the National Day of 1973, the Taiwan compatriots were referred to as "blood brothers," and there was a greater feeling of warmth and intimacy. Although this was only a verbal embellishment, it comforted Xiangdong considerably. Not long afterward he heard people say that this expression had been added because Premier Zhou had received a suggestion from a Taiwanese who had returned on his invitation. It was also said that this Taiwanese had even been an ardent supporter of the Taiwan Independence Movement, which was considered a counterrevolutionary group by the state. No one knew whether this rumor was true or not, but it made one think. Xiangdong often asked himself what, after all, was the best way for overseas students to make a contribution to their homeland.

Xiangdong sighed deeply. A lone star seemed to be staring mutely down at him. The night wind was rising, and growing colder with each gust. The farm dormitory stood in silence, most of its lights extinguished. Xiangdong's watch read nearly half past ten, time for him to go on duty. He hurried to the duty office, which was to the east of the dormitory, alongside the agricultural equipment storeroom. Yellow light streamed through the closed windows. Xiangdong pushed open the door and went in. Lao Fu was sitting under the light, carefully cutting open an empty tin can. On the table beside him were an unfinished kerosene stove, an awl, a round mallet, and several other tools.

"Hey, Xiao Liu," Lao Fu muttered as he peered over his glasses, his hands manipulating a pair of shears.

Xiangdong returned his greeting and sat down across the table from him. They had shared night duty once before; on that occasion, too, Lao Fu had kept himself busy making kerosene stoves. The stoves had earned Lao Fu quite a reputation in the school and had made him a very popular man. It was said that he had made more than a dozen during the latter part of the Cultural Revolution and had given them all to the people who needed them most.

"Since you've successfully completed your stint under the May Seventh Directive and will be leaving tomorrow for Nanjing, I'll treat you to my home-cooked noodles with eggs." Lao Fu spread out the open tin can on the table and began flattening it with the mallet.

"You treated me last time, so tonight it's my turn," said Xiangdong, opening one of the desk drawers to look at the noodles and eggs that had been placed there earlier. There was also a copy of Lenin's works.

"All right," Lao Fu agreed, "but since I have all the other ingredients, I'll do the cooking."

He was, after all, still the one who thought of everything. Xiangdong was embarrassed, for he had forgotten all about the condiments and other necessary ingredients. He took out the book and closed the drawer. Lao Fu began to punch holes in the piece of tin, pounding intently. Xiangdong's eyes followed every movement of the awl; with each punch another hole appeared, always the same size, very quick and neat.

Upon his arrival at the farm Xiangdong had heard the story behind this craft of Lao Fu's. Lao Fu had been a talented student at Central University who subsequently joined the teaching staff there not long after Liberation. He'd quickly risen to the position of senior lecturer, and on the eve of the Cultural Revolution had been a nominee for the position of associate professor. Unfortunately, toward the latter part of the Cultural Revolution, at the very beginning of the Cleansing of the Class

Ranks,* someone had sent in his name as a suspected member of the Three Principles of the People Youth Corps† while still a student at Central University. He was also accused of lying about his age. The leadership, following its policy of "better to believe that there is than there is not," formed a special committee to begin an investigation.

Two years passed without unearthing any evidence against him. The four or five members of the special committee took turns going to his hometown to investigate, and also went to other provinces to interview some of his old classmates; but they turned up nothing. Yet even with no actual proof that he had participated in the Youth Corps, they dared not let him go, so he was kept "dangling" indefinitely. Naturally, as the accused, he was the only one who suffered. During the "Cleansing" period he was jailed for six months and was then sent to a term of supervised labor. Finally, along with all the other teachers of the university, he was dispatched to northern Jiangsu to establish the May Seventh Cadre School farm.

Since then the One Attack, Three Antis,‡ anti–Lin Biao, and other campaigns had been launched one after the other, and the school had had no time to pay any attention to Lao Fu. The whole affair was left unfinished, and the political hierarchy seemed to have forgotten that he ever existed. Meanwhile, he remained optimistic, always good-natured and even-tempered, and never despaired. His wife, however, had tried to kill herself.

---

*Cleansing of the Class Ranks (*qingli jieji duiwu*), the purging of those who did not follow Chairman Mao's revolutionary line.
†A Nationalist organization based on Sun Yat-sen's Three Principles of the People.
‡One Attack, Three Antis (*yida sanfan*), a campaign launched in 1970. The One Attack was against the counterrevolutionaries; the Three Antis targeted corruption, waste, and opportunism.

She'd been investigated three or four times and hadn't heard a single word from her husband (nor, for that matter, had she been told what crime he may have committed). In desperation she threw herself into the river, but luckily she was rescued. When Lao Fu received word from his relatives, he did not betray the slightest emotion. If the officials in his hometown hadn't notified the authorities at the school that his guilt-ridden wife was under suspicion for having attempted suicide, no one in the school would have known about it.

While he was in isolation and under investigation Lao Fu became interested in making kerosene stoves. He first remade the one he'd been given to use. Then during his labor reform period he searched out old empty tin cans wherever he could find them, and cut and pounded them whenever he had a little spare time. While his hands were thus occupied, he was oblivious to everything going on around him.

"Say, Lao Fu, I heard some of your colleagues talking, and it seems that the school is considering setting you up with some classes this fall." Ever since hearing Lao Fu's story, Xiangdong had been very sympathetic toward the older man. He'd looked forward to reporting this bit of news.

He never dreamed that Lao Fu's response would be a disinterested "Is that so?" Lao Fu's eyes never left his hands, as he continued to poke holes. Xiangdong gazed at his hunched back and his bent head, the prematurely white strands of hair catching the light. He could restrain himself no longer.

"You've been a teacher for so many years," he said compassionately. "Don't you feel that you're wasting your talents, spending all your time working on the farm and making kerosene stoves instead of being in class?"

"I rather like living on the farm," Lao Fu answered, this

time putting down his work. He raised his head and looked at Xiangdong through his glasses, a half smile on his face. "And as for waste, you talk as though there were only a few things being wasted!"

How true! thought Xiangdong.

"I think the farms should be shut down," Xiangdong said frankly. "In the future, when there are more students, how will they be able to spare the teachers? Besides, it's a financial loss! None of the other socialist countries—even our beloved Albania—ever did this. Having every university set up a collective farm is a waste of manpower and resources."

"The Chinese Communists have always done what others before them have never done," Lao Fu stated solemnly. Then he smiled. "And as for losing money, that isn't even worth mentioning. During the past three years we've lost more than thirty thousand a year, and that's only the investment in seeds, fertilizer, and agricultural equipment; it doesn't include the teachers' pay. Just think: we have an average of one hundred people on the farm, and a year's produce can only feed these people for six months. So how can we avoid losing money? And that doesn't take into account what's been stolen."

Xiangdong frowned, as he recalled that on his arrival at the farm the committee chairman had held a meeting to decide on the night duty schedule. The need for a night watch had come as a great shock to Xiangdong: Chairman Mao had ordered the teachers to come and learn from the poor and lower-middle class peasants, and since they were to be surrounded by these people, what was the purpose of the patrols? But there had been a duty watch every night, and the strongest men had been chosen for this assignment. As a result there was never enough labor in the fields to finish the work. Yet, even with these precautions, thefts often occurred, until even Xiangdong felt let down. At this point in his thoughts, he seemed to hear the dry laugh of the young peasant at dinner.

"Intellectuals need to participate regularly in labor," Xiangdong stated emphatically, "but the universities really needn't carry the load of a large farm."

"Chairman Mao said, 'The May Seventh Directive should go on forever,'" Lao Fu quoted in even tones. Then he picked up his awl and started punching holes again. "His many years of revolutionary experience have taught that only labor can change one's thoughts."

Labor, labor—Xiangdong mulled the word over, suddenly feeling that it was meaningless. Aside from posing for photographs, he thought, it must be years since Chairman Mao has touched a rake, yet he alone has kept his youthful revolutionary spirit and is still going strong at his age. He must have a secret, thought Xiangdong, and it pained him that Mao was unwilling to share it with the people. A pity! Sighing deeply, Xiangdong stood up, and, with his arms behind his back, began to pace around the duty room. Tap! Tap! The sound of Lao Fu's awl hitting the tin plate was dry and monotonous. Xiangdong tried his best not to look at him or listen to that empty sound. He looked up and began counting the beams: one, two, three . . . , one, two, three . . .

"Shall we go make a round?" Lao Fu had stopped working and was rubbing his eyes.

Xiangdong looked at his watch. It was precisely midnight. He took a flashlight out of a drawer in the desk. Lao Fu put on a blue cloth cap and threw a tattered padded jacket over his shoulders. Then he opened the damper of the stove in the corner of the room and put some water on to boil. He picked up another flashlight and walked out with Xiangdong.

"Hm, the weather's changed. The wind's picked up."

Xiangdong never realized that the weather in northern Jiangsu could change so fast. The moon had set, and the sky had become an expanse of black; and the chill wind was whistling loudly.

The men walked past the two rows of dormitories on the right, and then along the rice paddies. They inspected the animal shed, the threshing grounds, and the barn; then they circled the broadcasting room, the office, the kitchen, and the dining hall and finally headed back to the duty office.

"All's quiet," Lao Fu remarked lightly, as he hung up his cap and jacket. He began to cook the noodles. In his years of living alone, he had become quite a hand at cooking, and his movements were quick and sure. Xiangdong handed him the eggs and noodles, and then just stood by and watched him as he worked.

"You people have been pretty lucky these past three months. You've only lost some meat, a little bit of fish, and a few *mantou*," said Lao Fu, as he prepared the noodles. "The autumn before last, in one night we lost seven bags of rice, each one weighing between one and two hundred catties. That was the worst time. In the morning they discovered the barn door half open and some wheel marks on the ground; that's all they found."

"Do you mean to say," Xiangdong gasped in disbelief, "that the thieves used a cart and that more than one person was involved? Did they find out who stole the rice?"

"Find out?" scoffed Lao Fu. "The incident was reported to

the County Guard Section, and they sent people over to investigate. And the farm's Party secretary and chief administrator spent the better part of a day with them, but no official report was ever issued. From then on, such incidents always went unreported."

Xiangdong was speechless. Thrusting his arms behind his back, he again began pacing beside the table. But Lao Fu quickly produced two bowls of noodles and coaxed him into sitting down to eat with him. Although the ingredients were quite ordinary, Lao Fu's handiwork had produced a very tasty dish. Xiangdong insisted on washing the dishes, and by the time he'd finished cleaning up, Lao Fu was cutting out another piece of tin. Xiangdong looked at the gray hair on the man's temples and smothered a sigh. Then he sat down opposite him and opened the book of selections from Lenin.

But he could not concentrate. He read two pages without having the slightest idea of what it was all about. He envied the way Lao Fu was able to concentrate on his work.

"Before . . ." Unable to restrain himself, Xiangdong began to question the other man again. "I mean to say, before the Cultural Revolution, what did you do in your spare time?"

Lao Fu looked at him curiously, then glanced at the book in his hands, and said coldly, "I read books."

"Is that so?" Xiangdong unconsciously responded in the same tone of voice.

Lao Fu stared at him, then lowered his head and continued with his cutting. After a moment he began to speak again, nonchalantly, as if he were talking about someone else's past. His head remained bent over his work as he talked. "I used to love books. Aside from the books of my trade, I especially loved literature and history. My father had studied literature and left me a great many books. Then since I was an avid book-buyer myself, I collected some eight or nine hundred volumes. At the beginning of the Cultural Revolution, during the tearing down of the 'four olds'—old culture, old customs, old habits, and old thoughts—I burned all my old copies of the traditional books. Afterward, as the new writers started to fall, one by one, I didn't have the time to sort them out, so I just borrowed a wooden cart and took the whole lot to the garbage station and sold them as waste paper for four fen a catty. Since then, except for *Mao's Selections*, I haven't bought a single book."

Xiangdong couldn't say a word. A picture he'd often seen in TV documentaries flashed across his mind: Chairman Mao receiving foreign visitors, and behind him bookcases filled with books, all valuable treasures.

Books, books. He abruptly pushed away the one in front of him and stood up. Tap! Tap! Lao Fu was punching holes again, monotonously, mechanically, endlessly. Xiangdong put his arms behind his back once more and again started pacing across the small room. He was so upset that he wanted to stamp his foot with all his might, although he knew it wouldn't help matters. He could only retrace his footsteps, back and forth, hopelessly.

"Why do I read books?" he suddenly asked himself. If Chairman Mao is the only one left in the entire country who reads and collects books, then what sort of future is there for Chinese culture? And what has the Cultural Revolution done to culture? A whole string of questions crowded his mind, until his head felt like bursting, while his heart felt empty. He stuck his face against the windowpane to cool his hot cheeks and lost all consciousness of place and time. In the midst of his confusion he seemed to hear a dog barking. He lifted his head. The light, Lao Fu, the kerosene stove—they immediately pulled him back to reality. He was instantly on the alert.

"I heard the cook's dog barking," he said to Lao Fu. "Shall we go take a look?"

"The dog's barking? All right," Lao Fu agreed unenthusiastically, as he put down his work.

Xiangdong picked up the flashlight. "I'll go to the right, you go to the left, and we'll meet at the dining hall."

He opened the door and ran out. The night was dark, and the wind was blowing. He switched on the flashlight and walked briskly toward the dining hall. Except for the sound of his own footsteps, there was a deathly silence all around him. He began to wonder if he'd been overly nervous and had mistaken the sound of the wind for a barking dog. He flashed his light on the dining hall door and saw that it was still locked, and as he swept his flashlight past the windows, he could see that they were all tightly closed.

He went around to the kitchen, in the rear. The cook's dog growled softly at the flashlight, but when it recognized Xiangdong it began to wag its tail. Xiangdong flashed his light on the windows and discovered that one of them was open a crack. At the same moment he heard something heavy hit the ground. He ran to one of the windows and peered inside the kitchen. Yes, the opposite window above the stove was also open. He quickly turned around and ran in that direction, but before he got there a shadowy figure started running toward the vegetable field. There really was a thief! At first Xiangdong was startled, then he got angry. Without even thinking, he began to chase the thief, pointing the flashlight at the retreating shadow.

The running figure was very tall, and must have had strong legs. Xiangdong clenched his teeth and ran as fast as he could;

he seemed to be gaining, but he couldn't catch the man. The thief burst across the vegetable field into the potato patch. At the end of the patch, he slipped and fell into a large ditch. He immediately got back to his feet, but just before falling, he'd looked back, and in the beam of the flashlight Xiangdong had recognized his large round face and heavy eyebrows. Xiangdong stopped dead in his tracks, almost dropping the flashlight.

He stared straight ahead, into the darkness. The wind began whistling again, blending with the sound of his labored breathing. Then he heard the dog barking again. It must be Lao Fu chasing over with the dog. He started to walk back, carefully shining his light on the potato patch, picking his way along the ditch. He met Lao Fu and the dog at the edge of the vegetable field.

"Did you see anything?" asked Lao Fu.

Xiangdong shook his head. His heart was pounding. "It looked like a black silhouette. I chased it for a while but I didn't see anything."

There was more he wanted to say, but his mouth was parched. He hoped that Lao Fu wouldn't pursue the matter. He was relieved to hear Lao Fu say, "A thief who comes to the kitchen could only be trying to steal something to eat. Let's go. We'd better wake up the cook so he can see if anything's missing."

Residency
Check

I didn't know Peng Yulian very well. Although we were close neighbors—my bedroom window faced hers and the front door of her apartment—we had no opportunity to chat because we worked in different units. On those occasions when we did meet on the way to and from work, she always smiled warmly, exposing her white, even teeth and looking at me with moist, glistening eyes. I could not help meeting her glance and answering her smile with one of my own. The old women who lived in the university dormitory called her a siren behind her back, most likely because they were jealous of her captivating eyes.

As far as we women were concerned, Yulian was by no means a beauty, and was, in fact, very short. But since she took such good care of herself and was very particular about what she wore, her figure always appeared well proportioned. Her breasts, large and curvaceous, attracted immediate attention. She always had her hair cut and blown dry at the large hairdresser's near the Drum Tower, and although she wore it in the same bobbed fashion as everyone else, hers was always nicely fluffed, in what the girls called the "Shanghai style." Her skin was dark, her nose was a little flat, and she had a large round face that didn't seem to suit her small stature. But her eyes were big and bright and so expressive that when she looked at you, they held all manner of allurements. Men were captivated by her, so naturally many of the women looked upon her with envy and malice.

The first time I actually talked with her was on a winter morning soon after I moved into the compound. We were pushing our bicycles out our front doors at the same time that day, and we had shopping baskets hanging from the handlebars. She called out good morning to me, I returned her greeting, and we rode together to the market. The weather was terribly cold, and I was bundled up in a padded jacket, padded trousers, padded shoes, a fur-lined coat, and a snow cap. I was wearing so many layers of clothing that it was a real effort just to get on my bicycle. But Peng Yulian was wearing only a pair of Shanghai-made maroon woolen slip-on shoes with flaps over the insteps; navy blue woolen trousers, a gaily patterned silk padded jacket, closely fitted so as to show off her figure; a maroon woolen cap; and black gloves. With the snow-covered ground as a setting, she looked particularly lovely and enticing.

It takes a lot of nerve to wear such bright colors, I thought.

Our breath was turning to mist, and I commented, "I never thought that Nanjing winters would be so cold!"

"I never did like Nanjing," she said frankly. "It's freezing cold in the winter and stiflingly hot in the summer. Now Shanghai has a nice climate. If you have a strong constitution you can get through the winter nicely with only a heavy sweater."

I surmised from these exaggerated words of praise that she was from Shanghai. People from Shanghai always seem to have a superiority complex, and to this day the Communist Party has been unable to transform it.

"What a mean bunch they are!" she suddenly blurted out, as she stomped down heavily on the pedal. "They *would* choose a snowy night to come around and make their residency check! Did they check you out last night too?"

"Yes."

I shivered, just thinking about the night before, when I had crawled out of a warm bed to be interrogated, and then got back into a cold bed with icy hands and feet.

"They come to my place every time they have one of their residency checks; their mothers' . . . !"

That was the first time I'd ever heard a woman utter this classic curse. I lowered my head and dared not look at her.

I too was fed up with residency checks. There was little anyone could say if they checked every household, but on those occasions when a random check was held, only a few families in each building were picked out. People claimed that anyone who is a problem case is checked every single time. My apartment was one of those that was always checked, but no matter how much I resented it, I didn't dare complain.

"I wonder why they had another random residency check last night," I said.

"What else, except they found themselves with nothing to do after dinner?" she said with a sneer. "According to the people who work in the clock factory, Nixon is on his way to Beijing, and public safety measures are being taken everywhere. It would seem that those public safety measures have reached all the way down to us."

By then we had arrived at the marketplace, and since there was such a crowd of people there, neither of us felt like talking any more. We parted company and lined up to buy food.

Following that first meeting, 1 took special notice of Peng Yulian because of her husband, Leng Zixuan. They seemed to be an unlikely couple. First of all, there was a marked disparity in their ages. Although Yulian was approaching her middle years, in general appearance and in the way she made herself up, she was holding on to her youth. Her husband gave quite the opposite impression, and seemed to be on the decline. It was said that Leng was not yet fifty, but his face was already deeply furrowed and half his hair had turned gray. He was bald around the temples, and his receding hairline left a broad expanse of forehead. Although he wore glasses, he was so terribly nearsighted he'd hunch his back and thrust his head out whenever he wanted to see something. In sharp contrast to his wife, he hardly ever smiled, and he was so reticent that he shied away from greeting any of his neighbors. The blank, far-away expression on his face always gave me the impression that he had some knotty problem on his mind.

One summer day just before evening fell, I caught a glimpse of him through the window. He was standing outside, leaning against his front door, and looking blankly up into the sky. His mouth was open and he was absolutely motionless, like some kind of fossil. Only when his daughter, who had come out to call him to dinner, tugged at his jacket, did he snap out of it. He lowered his eyes, adjusted his glasses with one hand, and stared at his daughter with a puzzled look.

He was an old man, no question about it, and I felt a little sorry for Yulian. But during the first year that I lived in the dormitory I saw Leng Zixuan only a few times, since he spent most of the time away performing manual labor.

The very day that I moved in, the secretary of the Party committee in my department came over especially to acquaint me with the political status of my neighbors. She mentioned Leng Zixuan again and again, calling him an "old-time right-ist." Later I occasionally overheard my fellow teachers refer to him as an "old political target," for he had been attacked in several political campaigns. He had been in detention for over a year in conjunction with the Cleansing of the Class Ranks and had also been found wanting during the recent One Attack, Three Antis campaign. This latest misfortune had come about in a most peculiar manner: One of the teachers—no one knows who—had written "Chinese Communist Party" on a piece of scratch paper, and Leng had added the word "dogs." Someone had retrieved the crumpled piece of paper from the wastebasket and forwarded it on up, and as a result one more account had to be settled on top of all the others. Reeducation through labor was ordered, and so an associate professor became a standing member of the May Seventh Cadre School labor force, which kept him away from home from then on.

But the incident that really aroused my interest in Peng Yulian occurred in the summer of 1972. One evening Zhou Min, who worked in my department, called on me and asked me to go with her to a meeting of the neighborhood com-mittee. Besides being colleagues, we lived in the same building. I spent quite a bit of time with Zhou Min because I liked her kind, gentle ways.

"What kind of meeting is it this time, Xiao Zhou? If it's another planned parenthood meeting, I'm not going. I've already been to several of those, and I've filled out all the required forms."

"No, that's not it," she said with a giggle. "This time it's about the Pan Jinlian* affair."

"Pan Jinlian?"

"I'm talking about your *honorable* neighbor, Peng Yulian."

She pointed through my bedroom window, then hurried me along. "Come on, let's go. You'll find out what it's all about when we get to the neighborhood committee meeting."

The meeting was being held in another building, in the apartment of a carpenter named Chang. Since Mrs. Chang didn't work she regularly served as the committee chairwoman, and every time there was a meeting she kicked her husband out of the apartment.

By the time we arrived the room was already filled with women, and as I looked around I saw that all of the Lengs' neighbors were there; every block representative was in attendance, even tottering old Guo Nainai and Shi Nainai. The room was buzzing with their chatter. Zhou Min and I found seats on the corner of the bed. I finally realized that they suspected Peng Yulian of having an extramarital affair and were discussing ways of keeping her under surveillance.

"Do they have any proof?" I turned to ask Zhou Min.

"Proof?" Shi Nainai, who was sitting in front of me, turned around. "We have all kinds of proof! There have been several eyewitnesses. With my own eyes I once saw a man slipping away from her place early in the morning. Ptui! What a piece of

---

*The notorious heroine of the sixteenth-century novel *Jin Ping Mei*, who was something of a nymphomaniac.

trash! Another time someone was seen sneaking into her place in the middle of the night. You just know he had to be up to no good. That shameless hussy doesn't even give a thought to the fact that she has a ten-year-old daughter!"

It came as no surprise that Shi Nainai should speak so harshly of Peng Yulian, for she had been widowed as a young woman and had raised two sons by herself. One of them had joined the army and the other was a Party member, so among all the people in our dormitory compound she was the most highly respected. It was only natural that she could not tolerate the slightest moral lapse.

"She is shameless, all right!" seventy-year-old Guo Nainai railed. "While her man is out performing manual labor, she is blatantly carrying on with other men. How will she ever be able to raise a daughter like that? Every time I see her all made up like some kind of demon I just want to throw up!"

"You said it!" Zhou Min added critically. "Her outlandish clothing has already been criticized several times, but she'll never learn her lesson and change her ways!"

"Change her ways? Why, she's out there flaunting herself in front of us!" Shi Nainai added with considerable spirit. "Do you all remember last summer when she wore that transparent pink silk blouse? She was wearing her brassiere so high that her breasts swayed and jiggled as she swaggered back and forth in the compound. Yan Nainai was making some comment about it to her when she cut her short and mumbled that big breasts are for men to suck on. Just imagine saying a thing like that! Poor Yan Nainai was so embarrassed she blushed all over and was almost in tears as she walked away."

"Didn't Chairwoman Chang also criticize her clothing

once?" A woman who lived next door to Peng Yulian seized the moment to denounce her. "She didn't dare talk back to her face, but the moment the chairwoman stepped out the door, she started to bellow, 'You expect me to start dressing up like a widow before my old man is even dead!'"

Chairwoman Chang's temper flared up. "If we don't straighten her out," she said, "the moral atmosphere of the whole dormitory will be destroyed. And if the young girls follow her lead!" She clapped her hands to get everyone's attention and called the meeting to order.

"Mei Laoshi,"—I never dreamed that I'd be the first person called on—"your place is directly opposite hers. Have you noticed any indiscretions?"

"Indiscretions?" I was caught completely by surprise, and since the place was filled with people, I began to stammer. "I'm . . . not aware of any."

"The reason we asked you here today was to discuss ways of catching her just once," the chairwoman stated. "Your window is opposite hers, which means you can see and hear anything that goes on inside. So we're going to rely on you to keep this area covered."

I couldn't do that, but I didn't dare refuse. While I was pondering my dilemma, Zhou Min poked me in the back, so finally I grudgingly acquiesced to their request.

"That's fine," the chairwoman said in a louder tone of voice, as she looked over the crowd of people with satisfaction. "That takes care of her front door, and we have Shi Nainai and the others to keep an eye out in the rear. Now we have to come up with the specific steps to be taken."

"This is what I would do," said Guo Nainai, who was always

very verbal during meetings despite her advanced age. "The moment we see a man entering her house, we go to the university security section and have them make a search. Then once we've caught her we can hold a big group session and soundly criticize her!"

This met with unanimous approval. Suddenly Zhou Min asked, "What if she refuses to open her door?"

"That's right," the chairwoman said, her resolve beginning to waver. "We must have an excuse for going into her house."

"How about a residency check!" someone shouted out.

"Good idea!" several people agreed, applauding.

"Who would dare refuse to open her door for a residency check?"

The plan of action was thus decided: Anyone who saw a man entering Peng Yulian's place was to make an immediate report to the neighborhood committee, which would post sentries at the front and rear. Then they would place a call to the university security section and ask them to send someone to catch the adulteress.

At this point the meeting should have come to an end, but since Peng Yulian was such a notorious figure, once we began talking about her we couldn't stop. We all seemed to have forgotten our fatigue after a hard day's work, and we were concerned only that we not miss a single tidbit of news. We craned our necks and cocked our heads as we listened intently. I had never been very clear on the Peng Yulian matter to begin with, and now here I was with the assignment of keeping watch over her. Naturally, in order to gain a true understanding of the person under my surveillance, I sat there from start to finish, taking in every comment, no matter how casual.

I discovered that this wasn't the first time she'd gotten into trouble. Back in 1963, during the Four Cleansings campaign,* Leng Zixuan had gone with his labor group to Sheyang county to participate in the Three Togethers movement—eat together, live together, and labor together with members of a commune. Before long, the Party secretary of his department, Ma Sui, began hanging around Peng Yulian on the pretext that it was his duty to look after the welfare of the members of his department. This Ma Sui was good-looking, fair, and had a real gift of gab, so Peng Yulian soon fell under his spell and into his grasp.

At the time, all her neighbors could see what was going on, but since Ma Sui was, after all, a Party secretary, no one dared breathe a word about it. At first he would just come over for a secret rendezvous and leave after they'd had their fun. But as time went on he grew more brazen and would actually spend the night at the Lengs' house when Mrs. Ma was out of town on an assignment. The affair became common knowledge throughout the dormitory district, and even Mrs. Ma got wind of it, though she never let on. The neighbors were incensed by the whole sordid affair, to say the least, but no one had the heart to tell Leng Zixuan.

After finishing with Peng Yulian, Ma Sui took up with the wife of the boilerman at the school. But they did not handle themselves very discreetly, and they were discovered by the woman's husband. A public uproar followed and Ma Sui was forced to make a formal written statement of self-criticism. The Party secretary of the school did everything within his power to hush up the scandal, but as luck would have it, his efforts were thwarted by the ushering in of the Great Cultural

---

*(*Siqing yundong.*) A campaign in which the people and the lower-level cadres were called upon to give a clean account of their political and ideological stand, family background, and financial situation.

Revolution. The boilerman joined the ranks of the rebels, and his wife came forward to denounce Ma Sui. He was ordered to make a clean breast of things, and when he submitted his confession, there was a resounding outcry. It turned out that he had been involved with a total of five women at the school, mostly teachers, including Peng Yulian; the methods he'd used and the details of the affairs shocked and disgusted the people.

During the outcry the streets were covered with wall posters denouncing Ma Sui, all the way from the school gate to the cafeteria, and they were pored over by a continuous stream of people. This was the first that Leng knew of the scandal involving his wife, and talk had it that within just a few days half his hair turned white and his walk became a shuffling gait, as though he had aged ten years or more. For the longest time he spoke to no one, and he acted like a mental incompetent. Some people were even afraid that he would try to take his own life.

"Didn't the two of them have a big fight or anything once the scandal was exposed?" I asked Zhou Min.

She smiled and said, "That's the strange part about it all. Shi Nainai has lived opposite the back door of their place for more than ten years, and she says she's never once heard them have an argument!"

"Really?" This puzzled me too. "But since the whole street was buzzing with the affair, I imagine Peng Yulian had to write a confession, didn't she?"

"A confession?" Shi Nainai turned around to break in on our conversation. "Don't even mention that 'confession' of hers! We had one talk after another with her, until our tongues nearly fell out, but all we were able to squeeze out of her was one page. Now I don't know how to read, so I didn't see it, but those who did weren't satisfied with it. You want to know why? Because she wasn't being truthful, that's why! She stubbornly protested that she was being wrongly accused, and that the only reason she'd had any dealings with Ma Sui had something to do with removing her husband's rightist label. According to her, falling into his hands had been unavoidable, and she said something about how it would have been harmful to her husband if she'd breathed a word to anyone about it. I think she was under the illusion that we would all go out and erect a memorial arch for her or something!"

Carpenter Chang walked in the door as she was saying her piece. We all looked at the clock. It was already past ten, so we quickly brought the discussion to an end and left.

One evening as I was walking home with my son, after picking him up at the day care center after work, I saw Peng Yulian riding her bicycle toward us. She had a large speckled hen in the nylon mesh bag on her handlebars. When she saw us she stopped and jumped to the ground.

"Why didn't you ride your bike today, Mei Laoshi?" she asked good-naturedly.

"One of my colleagues borrowed it," I answered with a smile.

She had a joyous look on her face, and she was composed, as usual. Her black, shiny eyes, even her dark skin, which was accentuated by her snowy white teeth, were attractive. She was wearing a pair of blue cotton slacks and a white Dacron blouse under a lightweight gold sweater. She didn't look all puffy like everyone else, but rather delicate and lively, and everything fit her just perfectly. Not only were the colors of her outfit well chosen, but even the way she wore her clothes was different. In Nanjing the women wore sweaters underneath their coats—no one wore them as outer garments. The talk had it that only factory girls from Shanghai dared to do that, and even in Shanghai they attracted a good deal of attention as they walked along the street. Peng Yulian showed a great deal of nerve in dressing so conspicuously and parading around in the dormitory district of a prestigious university. It was easy to understand why she was looked upon as an immoral person.

The moment my son spotted the chicken his eyes widened and were riveted on it. With a flurry of gestures, he began to shout, "Mommy, a chicken! A chicken!"

Feeling a little embarrassed, I was glad to take a cue from his words. "Where did you get such a big hen?" I asked.

"Someone from the Swallow Hill Commune brought some over to sell near our factory." She smiled again as she spoke. "Three-fifty apiece. I know that's pretty expensive, but it's a fine chicken and well worth it. My philosophy is to eat whenever the food's available. It's better insurance to store things in your stomach than to deposit the money in the bank, as some people do." She laughed, evidently pleased with her witticism. Then, seeing that the child's eyes were still on the chicken, she bent over and asked him, "Your name is Jingjing, isn't it? Do you like to eat chicken?"

He tugged at my sleeve. "Mommy, I want to eat chicken!"

Before I could say a word, Yulian turned to me and asked seriously, "Would you like one? You can have this one! It's no trouble for me to get them."

"No," I quickly demurred, "no."

"If not now, then perhaps I can get one for you the next time they come around."

I could see by her face that she wasn't making the offer just to be polite. Nonetheless, I momentarily lost my composure.

Shaking my head and making signs with my hands, I said, "No! No! I . . . I don't like chicken."

"Really?"

She stared at me incredulously. The smile slowly disappeared, and her face darkened. I avoided her eyes, as I felt my cheeks flush.

"Then let's just forget the whole thing," she said in an obviously forced tone. "So long, then. I'd better be going."

As I watched her ride off, I breathed a sigh of relief.

"Xiao Mei!"

I turned to see Zhou Min, who'd come up behind me during all of this.

"What's going on between you and Peng Yulian?"

I told her we'd met on the road and that she'd offered to give me the chicken. "She's quite a forthright and ingenuous girl, that one," I concluded aloud.

Zhou Min nodded. Then, in a low voice she said abruptly, "You wouldn't know, but she was once a model worker."

"A model worker?" I could scarcely believe my ears.

"That's the truth!" Zhou Min could not keep from smiling. After a moment she took my son's hand, and the three of us walked slowly to the dormitory. On the way she confided to me, "Outside of her fondness for prettying herself up and her extramarital affairs, there's nothing really wrong with Yulian. As for her family background, her father was a vegetable farmer in Minhang village near Shanghai, which makes him a member of the prestigious Five Red Elements. She joined the Communist Youth League as a young girl, and was on the point of being admitted into the Party when she was dismissed from the League because of her affair with Ma Sui."

"That's pretty severe punishment," I said.

"The Nanjing Clock Factory, where she works, took that action only after constant pressure by the rebel faction here at our school. At first they argued that since she'd been seduced, the blame should rest with the man, not with the woman."

"Do they know who the man is this time?"

Zhou Min shook her head. "According to Shi Nainai it's not someone from this area, so most likely he's from the clock factory."

"If they catch him, the people at the clock factory won't have any excuses this time around."

Zhou Min raised her eyebrows and said with a smile, "That's hard to say. The Nanjing Clock Factory can't fill the demand for their wristwatches, and since they can't meet production quotas as it is, why would they concern themselves with matters like this? Besides, the problem of relations between the sexes in factories is nothing new, unlike political questions, which can always be expanded and magnified. At most, it's nothing more than a decadent life style, and the worst that can happen is that they have to write out a confession. But that Ma Sui affair was a moral outrage, and the people were incensed over it. They demanded that he be dealt with severely, and the university had no recourse but to report to the provincial authorities and request that he be demoted and take a cut in salary. Their request was denied by the provincial authorities."

"Why was it denied?"

"They said that even though the situation was bad, it couldn't be considered rape, since all the teachers and workers had gotten involved with him of their own free will. They considered it a matter of life style, which could be dealt with through education. Naturally, the university was put in the bad position of being unable to face up to its own people, so after much negotiating the provincial authorities finally transferred him to another university."

"Really, there doesn't seem to be . . ." I was going to say there was no such thing as right or wrong anymore, but I held back and said indifferently, "No wonder Yulian has done the same thing over and over."

"Xiao Zhou," I said, talk of Peng Yulian reminding me of her husband and how the two of them seemed so different, "don't you get the feeling that Peng and Leng aren't well suited to each other? She's still so full of life, and he looks like he's on his last legs."

"He has aged a great deal these last few years," Zhou Min said by way of agreement, though there was a sympathetic ring to her words. "You may not believe it, but in the past it was she who chased after him."

"Really!"

Zhou Min laughed when she saw how startled I was. But she quickly assumed a more serious air as she continued, "You couldn't know, but the Leng of the pre–anti-rightist campaign and the Leng of today might just as well be two different people! He was promoted to associate professor in 1967—I remember it distinctly, since that was the year I was sent here to teach. At the time his wife had been dead a year, and he had no plans to remarry. He met Yulian quite by chance at the home of one of his colleagues. She fell for him the moment she laid eyes on him, and she took the lead in getting him to go rowing with her at People's Park. In no time at all he was hooked, and the two of them were constantly together. Three months later they were married."

"Incredible!"

"Hai! Naturally, he was a totally different man in those days. He was quite spirited then. Just think, an associate professor in his early thirties! Why, he walked with such style, with his chest out. People even copied his way of walking. He'd been a star pupil at Nanjing University—it was called Jinling University then—and a young man of real brilliance. He excelled in everything, including poetry. But he had too high an opinion of himself, and he was awfully naïve. During the Hundred Flowers Campaign he took the slogans seriously and really blossomed out with attacks on the cultural and educational policies of the Communist Party and the government. As a result he was the first person in the school to be labeled a rightist element."

"Quite a . . ." I was about to say "typical bookworm," but I couldn't be so unfeeling, and so I just heaved a long sigh.

"There was a time when the people in his department entertained the idea of removing that label from him. But then his department head discovered that he'd written a poem that he called 'Snow,' a title that Chairman Mao had used, and had set it in the form of 'Spring in Qinyuan,' just as Mao had done. But the mood of Leng's poem was dismal and chilling, quite the opposite of Mao's. As far as everyone was concerned, Leng was purposely throwing out a challenge, intending it as a satirical attack on Mao Zedong. So not only did he not lose the label, but he was lucky he didn't find himself wearing it to the crematorium!"

"Did you see the poem?" My curiosity was aroused.

Zhou Min shook her head. "That Leng Zixuan isn't one to back down. Even though he wrote several confessions, he insisted that he'd only written what he saw and felt, and he steadfastly denied that any satire had been intended. Some people demanded that the whole poem be made public, but the department authorities weren't willing to have this unhealthy influence spread any further, so they kept it classified, together with his written confession. The entire department hotly criticized and discussed the affair for a while, even though hardly anyone knew the actual contents of the poisonous weed."

By this time we'd passed through the main gate of the compound, and, probably because we were within range of the eyes and ears of others, Zhou Min said nothing more on the subject. We said goodbye and each of us headed home.

One night soon after that my dreams were suddenly shattered by the sound of someone knocking on a door. I awoke and pricked up my ears. Sure enough, someone was knocking on the Lengs' door. That Yulian is sure a sound sleeper, I thought; the noise woke me but there wasn't a peep from her. Then I heard a man shout impatiently, "Open up in there! Residency check!"

Another residency check! Just hearing the words disgusted me, as I knew there would be no more sleep for me the rest of the night. Being nervous and a poor sleeper by nature, I found it next to impossible to close my eyes again if I awoke during the night. Since the residency check was sure to include my place, I figured I might just as well get up and wait for them so I wouldn't be flustered at the last minute, and also to prevent my son from waking.

I turned on the light, got dressed, dug out my residence documents, and sat in front of my desk by the window to wait. Just then the clock on the wall began chiming the hour—it was midnight, a typical hour for a residency check. I lifted a corner of the curtain to look outside. It was pitch black except for a light coming from the Leng apartment. Their front door was ajar, and I could see someone moving behind the window, but since a curtain separated us, I couldn't see clearly. I let my curtain fall back into place, and began to flip through a book.

As expected, in about the time it would take to drink a cup of tea, someone came knocking at my door. I walked over leisurely, opened the door, and with the same motion handed over my residence documents.

"Oh, pardon us, we're not here for a residency check." At this I grew uneasy. The first person through the door turned out to be Mrs. Chang, the chairwoman of the neighborhood committee. There was an unwonted look of apology on her face. She was followed by two men who belonged to the school security section and a woman whose face seemed familiar to me—most likely she was a member of one of the school workers' families.

"Here's why we've come," Chairwoman Chang was saying. "We suspect that Peng Yulian is up to something. Earlier this evening someone saw a man sneak into her place and did not see him come out. Just a while ago we entered her place on the pretext of a residency check but we didn't find a man inside. Yulian was red in the face, like a thief who's been caught in the act, but since she hadn't violated any law, we couldn't very well make her open up her trunks and cabinets so we could look through them. We think she hid him somewhere, so we've come to ask you to keep an eye on her and to be sure to report anything suspicious to the neighborhood committee."

There was nothing I could do but assent, and after a few more admonitions by the chairwoman, the four of them departed.

As if I had nothing better to do than meddle in things like this! Anger filled my heart as I undressed, turned off the light, and got back into bed.

But just as I had feared, after this ordeal, any chance of going back to sleep had vanished. I tossed and turned in bed, and like someone who has drunk a lot of strong tea, I grew more and more wakeful. That damned Peng Yulian! After all that tossing about in bed I couldn't keep from cursing her. Everyone in the neighborhood had to lie awake nights because she got herself into trouble! But then I thought of how she had been in imminent danger of being disgraced in front of everyone, and I ended up by being glad for her. But just who was the man? Here I was, living opposite her, and I'd never noticed an unfamiliar man entering or leaving her house. In a big dormitory like this, I thought to myself, with all these people living close together, there naturally were many tongues to wag. Who knows? Some gossip may have raised a false alarm, which started the people talking and gave rise to a groundless disturbance.

After giving rein to my thoughts for a while—I had no idea what time it was—I noticed the faint light of day coming in through the window, and then the shape of the window itself gradually became visible. Since sleep was out of the question, I decided to get up and get dressed, make myself some tea, and then amuse myself by writing in my diary.

I happened to pull back a corner of the curtain and glance out the window. Imagine my shock when I saw the Lengs' front door open slightly and without a sound. Then a head peeked out through the opening and looked left and right. It was followed stealthily by the rest of the body. With lowered head and hat pulled low, the figure tiptoed toward the rear gate of the compound. In my agitation I didn't get a good look at the person's face, but there could be no doubt that it was a man—I wasn't mistaken about that. The Lengs' door was already closed when I looked back; there were no lights in the house and the curtain was pulled down all the way. Suddenly one corner of the curtain was raised, and someone's face was pressed against the glass. The instant our eyes met we both withdrew and lowered the curtains as quickly as possible.

I remained standing beside the window for a long time, my legs rubbery, my hands clasped tightly together and pressed against my breast, as I tried to stop my heart from beating so wildly. If I live a hundred years, I'll never forget Peng Yulian's wide staring eyes. Was her look one of terror, mortification, or defiance? I shall never know.

Before the day was out, news of the Peng Yulian affair had spread throughout the school and the dormitory. By sheer coincidence, Zhou Min had risen early that morning and noticed a man with his hat pulled down over his eyes. She saw him walk very nervously toward the rear gate, open it with a key, and leave. When Chairwoman Chang came over in the morning for information, Xiao Zhou reported what she had seen. Actually, she hadn't seen which place he'd come out of, but everyone eagerly jumped to the conclusion that he was none other than Peng Yulian's lover. People said that the chairwoman recalled seeing a key lying on a table while the neighborhood committee members were making their residency check the night before. She surmised that Peng Yulian had hidden the man in the wardrobe, but in the excitement she hadn't had time to hide the key. Once Chairwoman Chang figured this out she stamped her foot and yelled, "What a shame!" But there was nothing to be gained by regret, and since they hadn't caught the culprit, naturally they had no case against Peng Yulian. She continued to ride her bicycle around the dormitory area in complete freedom, like someone without a care in the world.

The news inevitably reached the May Seventh farm in

northern Jiangsu. The farm closed down for a few days before New Year's, and on the eve of Leng's departure for Nanjing, his section leader called him in and told him about the affair. He advised him that if he wanted a divorce, the school authorities would be willing to consider his request since Peng Yulian had repeated her offense time and again.

But to everyone's surprise, Leng stated without any show of emotion, "If Yulian wants a divorce, I'll consent to it any time, but under no circumstances will I bring up the subject myself."

This bit of news became *the* topic of conversation. Some expressed wonderment and admiration for his "magnanimity," while others called him a spineless weakling who would not let go of a "worn-out shoe." Then there were those who gleefully predicted that it would be strange indeed if he didn't beat her within an inch of her life the moment the two of them were together!

But as it turned out, on the day that Leng arrived home, Yulian, her face beaming with joy, brought home an old hen, and as she plucked its feathers she was even humming to herself. Her neighbors kept their ears pricked up all night, waiting for the sounds of an argument that never came. At this point the school notified Leng that he was to teach a language course, so he no longer had to take part in manual labor. From then on I saw him often; sometimes he would be walking all alone in the schoolyard, while at other times he would be sitting next to the window in his quarters, lost in thought and looking up into the sky for hours on end. On my way to and from work I also ran into Yulian quite often, and she greeted me with a smile as always, but she never again stopped to chat.

Ren Xiulan

In the summer of 1971 Nanjing had plenty of rain, so the grass and shrubbery were exceptionally lush. As the supervisor of the Elementary Students Management Section, one of my main responsibilities was to supervise the children as they tended the lawn in front of our office.

I was one of three women teachers from the Hydraulic Engineering College who were in charge of over thirty children. Their parents—teachers and staff members of the school—were undergoing labor reform in northern Jiangsu in accordance with the May Seventh Directive, and as there were no grandparents in the families to look after the children, they were left in our care. Even with a relatively small number of children, we still had to take possession of six classrooms to house them and provide for their school work and their recreational needs. The row of rooms faced south, and the large plot of grass in front of it became our responsibility. Several heavy downpours since the beginning of summer had made the grass grow fast, and I had been chosen to see that the children cut the lawn every weekend.

One Saturday morning in early August, as the children and I were working in front of the building as usual, several of the fifth- and sixth-grade boys slipped away to play on Qingliang Hill, above us. The younger children continued to work cheerfully, talking and laughing as they weeded and cut the grass, some using their hands and others using scythes. By high noon everyone was soaked with perspiration, but the work was finished and everything was neat and clean. Just as we were putting our tools away, Ma Shifu* of the Workers' Propaganda Corps came running toward us, waving at me, oblivious of the sweat pouring down his face.

When I saw how upset he was, my heart leapt into my mouth, for I was afraid that the boys who had slipped off to the hill had gotten into some kind of trouble. Once before, when a student had fallen out of a tree while reaching for a bird's egg, Ma Shifu had rushed to inform me in exactly the same manner.

"Ma Shifu!" I hurried forward to meet him.

"Chen Laoshi, I've got to see you!" was all he said as he hurried toward our office.

I told the children to go wash their hands for lunch, all except the Wang sisters, whom I asked to dispose of the grass clippings. Then I anxiously rushed over to the office. Ma Shifu was nervously pacing back and forth. The minute I entered the room he shut the door.

"Ren Xiulan has run away!" he said abruptly, fiercely scratching the back of his head. He was very upset and seemed at a loss for what to do.

"Ren Xiulan ran away?"

No wonder he was so upset. Ren Xiulan was a former Party secretary at our school. She had been a fanatic "leftist" at the

---

*Shifu is a polite term for an artisan or laborer.

beginning of the Cultural Revolution, but she was now under detention in a "study class" after being indicted as a leader of the May Sixteenth counterrevolutionary group.* Her husband was a political secretary of one of the divisions of the Nanjing Military District and had been a well-known policy maker when the rebels first rose to power during the Cultural Revolution. However, when the present campaign began he was among the first group of people detained in the military district study classes. Among other crimes, his wife had been accused of acting as a liaison between the military and the university; she was said to be the local extension of the black arm of the Nanjing military counterrevolutionaries. It was, of course, a very serious matter if such a person ran away.

"Yes, she's gone!" Ma Shifu exclaimed as though he had been personally victimized; his wrinkled old face lengthened with anger. "It happened before eight o'clock this morning. She fooled us, saying she was going to the toilet, then she just disappeared."

But how could she have run away? The target of each study class was constantly surrounded by five or six people who "studied" together day and night, slept in the same room, ate together, and even went to the toilet together. Moreover, the windows of all the rooms were encased with wooden bars. With such close security, it was nearly impossible for her to escape, and of all places, from the toilet! Ren Xiulan's ingenuity was indeed almost supernatural, I thought.

"Wasn't the window of the toilet nailed shut?" I asked.

---

*(*Wuyiliu fangeming jituan.*) An ultra-leftist group that was said to be particularly opposed to Premier Zhou Enlai and the Ministry of Foreign Affairs. Leaders of this group were said to be important lieutenants of Jiang Qing during the Cultural Revolution.

"Aiya! I don't know when, but she loosened two of the wooden bars by pulling out the nails. Those guards are good for nothing but stuffing themselves with rice. God damn it!" Ma Shifu began to curse.

We were used to hearing curses from the members of the Workers' Propaganda Corps, even from such a kindly old man as Ma. He had previously been a janitor in the Nanjing Chemical Fiber Factory, but after being assigned to the Hydraulic Engineering College, he became as important as the Military Propaganda Corps members. But even with his high position he was always modest and good-natured, never putting on airs. At the meetings he would often bow to the people and say, "I've come to learn from you." He was the only member of the Workers' Propaganda Corps who was well thought of by one and all. The pity was that because he was illiterate and had no education, he was qualified only to manage production development. Our Elementary Students Management Corps was under his supervision, and teachers Yu, Xia, and I got along well with him, often asking for his advice.

"Ren Xiulan can't possibly get very far," I comforted him. "They're out to get all the May Sixteenth rebels, so she really has no place to hide."

"That's hard to say," he shook his head uncertainly. "There are too many May Sixteenth rebels in hiding. She didn't have her purse with her, so without money and ration cards she'll need help. After all, a rabbit can't grow a long tail!"

When I heard that Ren Xiulan had no ration cards I really began to worry about her. "Have you searched Qingliang Hill?" I asked.

"Of course, right away. But there wasn't a trace of her. That's why I've come looking for you. The hill is so large and so thick with trees and tall grass that several people could easily hide there. We just had a meeting and decided to have the students go up and search the hill."

That really took me by surprise. To take thirty or so children of various ages up to search the hill was a big responsibility. But then, how could I refuse the assignment? "No problem," I said, keeping my face expressionless.

Ma Shifu nodded apologetically. "I really shouldn't bother you three teachers, since you all have nursing babies at home, but we're short-handed. With over twenty study classes going on in the school, and Ren Xiulan running away, it's impossible to get anyone, especially since we've got to be doubly on our guard. We've also got to keep this a secret, because if the news were to reach the May Sixteenth confederates, there might be trouble."

He scratched his head again, and sighed deeply. "We're really desperately short of help. Every available person has already been assigned a job. Not only do we have to search up and down every street, but we've also got to send people to watch the train station and the docks. The whole school has been mobilized, and everyone in the Military Propaganda Corps has come out to join in the search. I think our Management Division should do its share, and since the children have nothing to do, let them look among the trees and in the tall grass. Maybe they'll find something before dark."

We agreed that we would wait until the children had finished their lunch. Then he would join us in going up the hill.

When the children heard that they were going to search the hill for a runaway they were very excited. Little Ming, the leader among the boys, immediately found some sticks to distribute among the bigger boys. The Wang sisters, not to be outdone, went to the dining hall and wheedled the cook into giving them some sticks for the girls too. Everyone in the school knew about Ren Xiulan, and there was a certain element of precocious seriousness in the children's excitement; even the first-graders behaved as though they were about to confront the enemy and talked to one another in whispers.

As soon as Ma Shifu arrived, the children rushed toward the hill like a swarm of bees, each of them struggling to be the first to get there.

"Form a line! Form a line!" Ma shouted hoarsely. "Proceed just like combing hair—don't miss a single spot! If you find anything, report it immediately."

With Ma Shifu at the eastern end and me at the western end, and the children between us, we formed an uneven twisting human line that slowly made its way up the hill.

The Hydraulic Engineering College had been built on the side of Qingliang Hill and, together with the Nanjing Crematorium, occupied half the hillside. Aside from the Military Division based at Tiger Pass, the rest of the hill was uninhabited, but since many people came to get firewood and farmers cut the grass to feed their animals, the area was not completely wild. That day, as we swept up the hill, the guards posted by the Liberation Army had been alerted to expect us, but several old men who were cutting grass watched us as we bent over and turned aside nearly every blade of grass. "What are you looking for?" they asked.

"We lost some money!" the children answered in unison.

"Money?" The old men squinted at Ma Shifu and me in obvious disbelief. However, they asked no more questions, and before long they gathered their things and left silently.

The Wang sisters were walking beside me, chattering incessantly, and as they searched through the grass, I overheard them discussing a girl named Shi Hong, who seemed to be related to Ren Xiulan.

"Who's Shi Hong?" I asked.

"She's Ren Xiulan's daughter."

I'd heard that Ren Xiulan's youngest daughter was a middle school student and had been a Red Guard leader. She was exceedingly active and quite well known. My curiosity aroused, I asked, "Do you know her?"

"Our oldest sister's her classmate!" the older one boasted. "She used to come to school in a jeep. But now she walks like a shadow and doesn't talk to anyone."

"Our oldest sister's teacher said that everyone must watch her because she might commit suicide."

Suicide! It was terribly unsettling to see a fifth-grade child talk of suicide without batting an eye.

"Even if her parents are May Sixteenth elements," I exclaimed, "it's got nothing to do with her as long as she takes a clear stand."

"They wanted her to denounce her parents, but she insists they are not May Sixteenth elements, and she won't back down. Our sister and her other classmates have even pasted up wall posters criticizing her."

She certainly is a worthy daughter of Ren Xiulan, I thought to myself. She's absolutely unyielding.

One of the Wang girls interrupted her searching to ask me solemnly, "Chen Laoshi, Ren Xiulan is a May Sixteenth element, isn't she?"

"Um,"—I wasn't at all sure myself—"probably so. Both the Workers' Propaganda Corps and the Military Propaganda

Corps publicly have declared her to be one, and they can't be wrong, can they?"

I was ashamed to give the child such an indefinite answer, but in truth I was confused about the May Sixteenth incident. In 1967, when I was in Beijing, I heard about a May Sixteenth Rebel Army Unit that had posted the slogan, "Aim a cannon at Premier Zhou" in Tiananmen Square. It had been removed almost immediately. Soon afterward, Jiang Qing herself had exposed several counterrevolutionary organizations, among which the May Sixteenth Rebel Army Unit was mentioned. But again, this had all been hushed up and in time forgotten. No one could have foreseen that after a few years, when the One Attack, Three Antis campaign was in full swing, the denouncement of the May Sixteenth group would resurface on orders from above. The May Sixteenth group was declared a left extremist organization, a bold and vicious gang of people who had dared to oppose Mao Zedong, openly attacked Zhang Chunqiao in Shanghai, and pointed a finger at Xu Shiyou in Nanjing. General Xu, vowing that he would "defend Mao Zedong's ideology to the death," swept through the military and the universities, eliminating the gang's members with a great hue and cry.

The people of Nanjing had been unaware of the existence of this group. It was only after the upheaval that they'd realized that it was this terrorist gang that had been behind all the murders, looting, and destruction during the Cultural Revolution. Nanjing was described as the main base of the May Sixteenth group, from which its influence had infiltrated the army and slowly spread throughout the whole nation. Since Nanjing is an important base of the Liberation Army, it was necessary to purge the city thoroughly of this evil.

As the purge got under way, many people were arrested in the military units, in the factories, and in the universities. Terror was rampant. According to an announcement by the Military Propaganda Corps of the Hydraulic Engineering College, the number of May Sixteenth elements in our school was in three digits, which meant that there were at least 100 and possibly as many as 999. Since there were only 1,000 or so in the entire school, people began to look suspiciously at one another, wondering if everyone else was a counterrevolutionary.

Nanjing University had been a model for all the colleges in Nanjing, and that was no less true during this campaign. I still remember vividly the first May Sixteenth Confession Meeting sponsored by the university. It was a hot day, and the sun shone fiercely on the more than twenty thousand people sitting in the huge, heavily guarded athletic field. One by one the May Sixteenth elements were forced up onto a high platform, where they were publicly accused. They then confessed amid tears and hysterical sobbing, some of them even fainting on the stage. Among the offenders was one who had been collecting incorrect sayings of Mao Zedong with the intention of using them for the "usurpation of power" when the time was right. There was a Red Guard who had taken a copy of Hitler's *Mein Kampf* while ransacking the library, and after studying the book thoroughly, he had made it his personal bible. There were also some who had been classmates for years, sharing the same quarters, and even some couples who had been married for over thirty years, who were completely unaware of each other's membership in this dreaded gang. The audience was badly shaken; I was dazed.

Was Ren Xiulan a member of the May Sixteenth gang? I really did not know—only Heaven knew.

We continued our search until dark, up and down the hill, without discovering anything suspicious. The children figured that Ren Xiulan had already fled from Qingliang Hill. Everyone was exhausted, and some of the smaller girls kept leaning against me. Ma Shifu decided to call it a day, so we headed back with the children.

The next morning, before we teachers could begin our daily study of the *Selected Writings of Chairman Mao*, Ma came running up to us. By this time Ren Xiulan had been gone for more than twenty-four hours. It was assumed that she'd had sufficient time to leave Nanjing, so the provincial government had telegraphed the security bureaus in her hometown in Shanxi province and her husband's hometown of Suzhou to put all her relatives under surveillance. Our college also sent people to watch the docks along both sides of the Yangtze River in case she tried to board a boat. The school authorities were afraid that her disappearance had been planned with inside and outside help, so they intensified security measures to prevent any further such happenings. Ma Shifu came to tell us that we must be especially careful to check out Qingliang Hill every day. "If you notice anything suspicious phone the office immediately." With this instruction, he rushed off.

"What a lot of commotion," Xia Laoshi exclaimed as she watched his retreating figure. "Ren Xiulan's disappearance has turned the school upside down. Look at the state Ma Shifu's in! He probably didn't get much sleep—his eyes are all bloodshot."

"Dr. Gu is the one to be sorry for," Yu Laoshi declared. "She was so upset she didn't even go home last night!"

"Why Dr. Gu?" Dr. Gu was a close neighbor of mine, but I wasn't aware that she'd been assigned to guard Ren Xiulan.

"That was changed this summer," Yu Laoshi informed me.

"Ren Xiulan has high blood pressure, but they suspected she was just putting on an act when she constantly complained of headaches and dizziness. Sometimes there wouldn't be a sound out of her for a whole day and night, and even thunder wouldn't have shaken her. They didn't know what to do, and they weren't sure whether her illness was real or feigned, so they finally reported the situation. The Workers' Propaganda Corps said this was easy to handle: all they had to do was assign a physician to be her guard and find out if she was pretending to be ill or not. So they put Dr. Gu in charge. Who would have thought that she'd be the one to land in trouble!"

I felt badly for the doctor, who was a good person, gentle and kind.

"There were so many guards around her," I protested, "they can't possibly put all the blame on Dr. Gu."

Xia Laoshi, who seemed to derive pleasure from seeing someone else in trouble, asked, "Well, why did she allow it to happen while she was on duty? She and Zhou were on night duty, and after they got up in the morning Zhou went to the dining hall to get breakfast. While she was making her bed, Ren Xiulan was given permission to go to the toilet and never came back. When Zhou returned with breakfast they discovered she was gone. Naturally, the responsibility was mostly Dr. Gu's."

"By coincidence, Dr. Gu once belonged to the Revolutionary Red Liaison group that Ren Xiulan supported, so this puts her in a very difficult position," Yu Laoshi added somewhat sympathetically. "Ren Xiulan couldn't possibly have loosened the nails from two wooden bars in a single day and night. They suspect that she'd been working on them for several months with her hairpin. The guards simply hadn't suspected a thing."

"She's really fast!" I said. "After climbing out the toilet window and running across the yard, she still had to make her way around the laboratory before she could go up Qingliang Hill. At most, she had ten minutes."

Ren Xiulan had been locked up in one of two small buildings on a little hill on the western side of the campus. These buildings had once been occupied by the Workers' Propaganda Corps when they first came to our school. Because they proclaimed that they were the true Marxist-Leninist representatives, who were spreading the thought of Mao Zedong, the place had come to be called Marx-Lenin Hill. It could not be considered an isolated area, as it stood next to the Hydraulic Engineering building and in front of the laboratory. It was unlikely that anyone could have run up to Qingliang Hill without being seen.

"You see, she's been a guerrilla ever since she was a child. She's known as the 'long-legged general,'" said Xia Laoshi.

"She's really something!" Yu Laoshi shook her head with a sigh, though there was an overtone of admiration. "She's been an old cadre member since the days in northern Shaanxi, and she's had plenty of experience in purging others. So although she's the one being purged now, it won't be easy to knock her down. She's probably the only woman ever appointed as Party secretary to a university in Nanjing."

"She's an old fox!" Xia Laoshi said. "At the beginning of the Cultural Revolution she sided with one group while attacking another, purging many rebel groups in the process. Now when the call is 'cadres step to the side' she's the first to fall. As far as I'm concerned, she's getting what's coming to her!"

Yu Laoshi gave me a meaningful look, and it suddenly dawned on me that Xia had once belonged to a rebel group that had been attacked by Ren Xiulan. No wonder she was so gratified by all this trouble. Every day we heard the slogan "eliminate factionalism," yet the roots of the different groups formed during the Cultural Revolution went too deep.

"You weren't here at the college when Ren Xiulan was at the peak of her fame, were you?" Yu Laoshi asked me, changing the subject.

I shook my head. Although Ren Xiulan was a notorious figure, I had seen her only a few times, and then only very briefly. The first time was when she passed by with a labor reform group, leading those still "unliberated" black elements in shouldering hoes on their way to work. A colleague had quietly pointed her out: "That older woman with the touch of gray in her hair is Ren Xiulan. She used to be a real sharpshooter; can you imagine that? In the old days she fought all over the Taihang Mountains. She joined the guerrillas when she was only fourteen and the Party at sixteen." I had looked at the short, stocky figure with increased admiration.

I saw her for the last time in the spring, when our school, following Nanjing University's example, called for a May Sixteenth Confession Meeting. It was attended by the entire school. All the May Sixteenth suspects were brought in; Ren Xiulan, the last to enter, was seated in the front row. I remember the way she walked in: calm, her head held high, her lips curled slightly in the semblance of a smile as her eyes slowly swept the hall with an unfaltering gaze. I imagined that must have been how she looked when she used to mount the stage to make reports to the school. But this time she looked much older; her face, no longer round, was wrinkled, and her hair was considerably grayer. She was also much thinner, unlike the others, who had grown plump and pale from a lack of sunshine and exercise.

"Ren Xiulan really used to have style," Yu Laoshi reminisced. "She often worked with us, wearing patched cloth shoes and a faded blue uniform. When we stopped for a rest she'd munch on a *mantou* without even washing her hands. I was deeply impressed until the Wang sisters' mother told me that her oldest daughter had been to Ren Xiulan's home—a large Western-style house with leather sofas and carpets on the floor, where even tea was served by an aide. So her simple austerity was just a show, put on for our benefit!"

I was about to express my feelings when Xia Laoshi hastily interjected, "Two-faced! Typically two-faced!"

Ignoring her, Yu Laoshi continued, "At one time Ren Xiulan advocated 'saving the country through physical fitness.' She organized ball games and a tai-chi boxing class for the female staff of the school, which I joined. You know, although she was short and plump, she was pretty good! She'd finish a whole set of boxing in five minutes without puffing or getting red in the face. Once we had a race and we all dropped out halfway through; all except for her, that is—she was the only one who finished a lap around the athletic field. She's really got strong legs. So I think that ten minutes would be enough for her to make her escape."

Talk of the race reminded me of what we were supposed to be doing. "The school has asked us to intensify our patrolling," I said, "so we'd better hurry and make some plans."

Xia Laoshi shook her head in disagreement. "I think it's useless. We've already been through all of Qingliang Hill like a comb several times. She must be out of Nanjing by now.

The minute they discovered she was missing yesterday they organized groups to search the hill and the laboratory, and the Military Propaganda Corps personally conducted a search of Marx-Lenin Hill. They turned over every blade of grass and went through the house where she'd been imprisoned, inside and out. They even opened up the cesspool outside the toilet and prodded it with a stick! I think she's already gone to Shanghai, where the black line of the May Sixteenth gang is stretched far and wide. Even worse, she may have joined our nation's enemies!"

In spite of all these speculations, we still carried out our instructions. We took turns leading the children up the hill daily, and we shook the trees and beat the grass. After a few days the children began to forget what they were there for, and most of them simply threw away their sticks and ran off to play. Finally, only the younger ones were left to return with the teachers.

By Friday afternoon nothing had been accomplished. The school was very quiet since almost everyone had been sent out on assignments. After seeing the children finish their dinner, I turned my duties over to Yu Laoshi and dragged myself wearily back to the dormitory. Halfway there I met Dr. Gu. It had only been a few days since I'd last seen her, but she was much thinner. Her eyes were sunken, her face was waxen and yellow, and she looked haggard.

"Dr. Gu!" I greeted her warmly, running up to grasp her hand tightly in sympathy.

"Chen Laoshi!" She placed her other hand over mine, looking at me with grateful eyes, which reddened even before she began to speak. "I really have rotten luck!"

"Don't worry, they'll find her," I said in a low voice. "They can't put the blame entirely on you; it's difficult to guard against this sort of thing."

She looked up and down the road to see if anyone was around. "I'm really unlucky. I've been here only two months, and already this has happened. By the time I came they'd already stopped following her to the toilet—that didn't start with me. Ren Xiulan is very cunning. She'd been shut up for over a year, but during these last few months she'd been on her best behavior. She didn't play any tricks, like fasting or pretending to be ill, and every day she'd study Chairman Mao's selected works before concentrating on her own writing. Everyone was relieved and began to relax. Who could have known she had secret plans! Aiya, what'll I do?"

I wanted to comfort her more, but she shook her head and pressed my hand tightly. "I've got to go to a meeting," she said, and walked off with her head bowed. My heart ached as I turned to watch her small, thin figure. At that moment I truly hoped that Ren Xiulan would be found soon.

The next day was Saturday again. Just as I was about to organize the children for some gardening, Ma Shifu walked up.

"Chen Laoshi, let's start all over again. We'll find her." He tried to sound optimistic but he couldn't hide his low spirits. "We had an emergency meeting last night. The reports have come in from everywhere—still no news. They believe that Ren Xiulan is probably still in Nanjing, possibly hiding in the western or southern part of the city, so they've directed us to begin the search all over again. This time we'll split up into separate groups and go over the grounds inch by inch. We'll dig into every hole and leave no stone unturned. The most important part is Qingliang Hill and the homes around that area—they'll be searched by the Military Propaganda Corps. You'll take charge of Marx-Lenin Hill. Begin right away, and I'll come help as soon as I finish giving the other groups their assignments." He then gave me two keys and left.

With the imprisonment of Ren Xiulan on Marx-Lenin Hill, the place had been declared off-limits to the children. So they were excited when they heard that they were to search there and went hunting for sticks again. I divided them into two groups: four or five older girls would search the inside of the house with me, while all the other children would search the grounds around it. Actually, no one had any hopes of finding a trace of Ren Xiulan, but the children were so curious about Marx-Lenin Hill they couldn't even wait to form a line. They dashed up the hill the minute I gave the order to go.

I took the Wang sisters and several other girls inside the four-room house where Ren Xiulan had stayed. Three of the rooms were furnished with tables, chairs, and benches. Two of them had evidently been used by the guards for their meetings, as the walls were covered with portraits of Mao Zedong and various rousing slogans such as "We Shall Not Give Up until the May Sixteenth Gang Is Vanquished!" "Pluck Out the Military Black Hand That Has Extended into Our School!" "Whoever Opposes General Xu Opposes Chairman Mao!" The third room must have been where Ren Xiulan's thought-reform sessions had taken place, since the walls were all covered with huge black characters and six-inch-long exclamation marks. The slogans exhorted her to "Bow Your Head and Confess!" and "Turn Back to the Shore!" One read "Even in Death There Is No Place to Hide!"

The fourth room had served as a bedroom for Ren Xiulan and her night guard. It had two windows but they were covered with black curtains. The room was so dark and gloomy that the girls were afraid to enter until I drew back the curtains, letting in the bright August sun. As in all the other rooms, five or six wooden bars had been nailed across the outside of the windows.

There were two wooden beds in the room. One was bare, while the other, probably Ren Xiulan's, still had a pillow and a quilt on it. Under the bed were two pair of shoes—one black leather, the other of quilted cotton. There was also a loose bedroll, which had obviously been searched many times. Several suits of ordinary cloth uniforms were piled on the two chairs between the beds, and a very old copy of Chairman Mao's selected writings was on the desk. The plaster walls showed scraps of recently removed posters, apparently torn down in such haste that some characters were still partly legible: "Dead-End," "Where to?" and the like.

We lingered awhile, touching this and that even though there weren't many things to be searched through. The children were disappointed, and got down on their hands and knees and looked carefully under the beds.

"Shall we take a look at the toilet, Laoshi?" one of the Wang sisters asked me.

"Yes, why don't we?" It took us a while before we found it, at the end of the veranda. I opened the door and went in first. Just then we heard loud shouts from the children outside the toilet window.

"Chen Laoshi! Hurry! Chen Laoshi!"

I dashed out, colliding with a child who was rushing inside at the same moment.

"Hurry, Chen Laoshi, hurry!" It was little Ming who grabbed my hand and pulled me around the corner of the house to a spot beneath the toilet window. The children were gathered in a tight circle, staring wide-eyed at something. Some of them were covering their noses, while several of the younger ones were hiding behind the others, their hands over their faces in fright. They quickly moved back to let me get a closer look. What I saw was the three-foot-square cesspool solidly filled with some object.

"Ren Xiulan!"

I don't know who called out the name, but the instant I heard it I became violently ill; a bolt of light flashed before me and I blacked out. I neither heard nor saw anything more.

I was sick for a whole week. I lay in bed not wanting to eat or drink, and every time I closed my eyes a black mass would float into my mind and I would become nauseated. Gradually I got better, and I realized that my reaction was not a physical one. A strong emotional chain was wrapped around my heart, and I would never in my life be able to unlock it.

Ma Shifu was very concerned about me and came to see me several times. He told me about the large criticism meeting that was held at the school. Many people had mounted the stage to denounce Ren Xiulan, declaring that she "began by pretending to be a leftist" and "ended by being an extreme rightist," that she "destroyed herself in the face of the people," and that her death "carried less weight than a feather." Naturally, her name would "stink down through the centuries." She was posthumously expelled from the Party and officially labeled a counterrevolutionary.

"If she wanted to kill herself by jumping into a cesspool, what could we do?" Even Ma Shifu sighed as he shook his head ruefully. "Just think, that cesspool is shallow—only about three feet deep—and not even as long as a person's body. If she hadn't squeezed into the corner, we'd have found her the first time we poked around in it. Ai! Why seek death? Dying like this is . . . how did they say it at the meeting? Oh, yes, 'carried less weight . . . less weight than a feather!' "

He was right.

That autumn the Lin Biao incident occurred,* and very soon it was full steam ahead with "Criticize Lin" and "Attack extreme rightists." Before a year had passed, all the May Sixteenth elements who had confessed publicly on the stages had recanted their confessions, claiming they had been coerced by torture and beatings. Many of their accusers were imprisoned and put into study classes as suspected Lin Biao followers. The alleged May Sixteenth elements in our school were gradually released—the last one being freed after three years of incarceration—and declared innocent of all charges.

The wheel of class struggle rolled on, and very soon May Sixteenth became a historical note in Nanjing, a memory of terror touched with absurdity. No one mentioned the death of Ren Xiulan any more, her name appearing only on the historical record of struggles at the Hydraulic Engineering College.

But for me it is different. Her death has been like an iron weight in my heart, sinking ever deeper.

---

*The alleged coup by Mao's right-hand man, and his subsequent death during an escape attempt.

The
Big Fish

Kuai Shifu came home early one February day. He popped his head inside the door and asked his wife, who was lying in bed, "How are you feeling? Any better?"

Mama Kuai had turned her head at the sound of the door opening, and now her face lit up at the unexpected pleasure of seeing her husband. She didn't want to worry him so she answered evasively, "Seems better. Doesn't hurt so much."

The windows and doors were tightly shut against the bitter cold, with wads of newspaper stuffed into the cracks. The odor of Chinese herbal medicine permeated the room.

"Have you taken your medicine?" Kuai Shifu asked as he glanced at the earthen pot on the small round table beside the bed.

"Yes, Zhang Sao prepared it. She even cooked lunch for me."

Mama Kuai's voice was filled with gratitude, even though the person who had done all these favors was not present. Her old backaches had recurred, and for the past few days she'd spent most of her time in bed. Without their neighbors' help, Kuai Shifu wouldn't have been able to go to work.

"Why are you home so early?" asked Mama Kuai, looking at the old clock on the wall near the foot of the bed. It was only three o'clock.

Kuai Shifu worked at the dockyards, some distance away. His work and his meetings usually kept him busy from morning to night, and since he had to change buses to get from the Yangtze River Bridge to Cockcrow Temple, he never got home before dark.

"This afternoon we were supposed to have political study, but they said some American newspapermen were coming to Nanjing, so at the last minute it was changed to a general clean-up. Those two apprentices of mine are really very thoughtful. They know you're sick and they wouldn't let me do anything. They practically forced me to go home."

As he talked, the old man took off his gloves and poured himself a glass of hot water from the vacuum bottle on top of the chest of drawers. He cupped his hands around the glass for warmth.

Mama Kuai smiled. "Those two young fellows seem to be all right. Let's just hope they won't turn out like the last one, who cursed you as though you weren't worth anything as soon as the Cultural Revolution began!"

The old man grinned as he sat down by the small round table. He blew on the glass of hot water before taking a tentative sip; finding that it was not too hot, he gulped it all down.

"What else could he have done under the circumstances?" he asked without a trace of resentment. "The campaign was in full swing and he had to take a radical stand if he didn't want to get in trouble himself. He felt sorry about it afterward, and he used to come when no one was around to apologize for what he did. At the time he thought about nothing but the revolution, so he neglected his work entirely. Now whenever he's in trouble, doesn't he always come running to me?"

"That's because you're so good-hearted!" Mama Kuai laughed. She was able to accept the incident now, but two years earlier, when she'd learned that the old man's apprentice had attacked him in wall posters, she'd been very upset. Especially disturbing was the fiasco of inviting the apprentice over for dinner one New Year's eve. It was entirely her idea, but the apprentice accused the old man of having ulterior motives, of going the way of the "imperialists," trying to "cultivate" and "corrupt" young workers. When the old man was subsequently forced onto the stage for "confession and criticism," the old woman seethed with anger.

"Speaking of my apprentices, I nearly forgot!" the old man exclaimed. "They said that during the welcome for the American newspapermen, for the next couple of days the markets will be better stocked than usual, especially the one on Dongren Street. They said you can get anything you want, so tell me what you feel like eating and I'll go get it for you."

The old woman closed her eyes and thought it over. Since she hadn't been to market for over a week, her husband had had to pick up what he could on his way home from work, and they'd eaten nothing but frozen cabbage for some time. It had been cabbage with soy sauce one day and cabbage with salt pork the next. The old woman was bothered by a bad stomach to begin with, and the monotony of the diet had robbed her of what little appetite she had left.

"I could go for a taste of fish soup," she said, her eyes brightening at the prospect. "It would be nice if you could get a fish.

Just think how delicious it would be, cooked with a few slices of ginger and some scallions. We could add a little bit of rice wine just before we eat it."

That was enough to make the old man's mouth water. "You want to eat fish? All right, you shall have it!"

He stood up and straightened his cotton-padded cap, which he hadn't removed after entering the house. Then he patted the pocket of his quilted jacket to make sure his money was there.

"I'll go to the Dongren Street market right away. My apprentices said they've got everything there."

He went into the kitchen, took a look at the stove, and was pleased to see a circle of blue flame underneath. He opened the bottom door a slit wider to get a little more ventilation, and picked up the market basket.

Kuai Shifu considered the distance between Cockcrow Temple and Dongren Street and decided to go by bicycle. It took him some time to get his bicycle out from under the bed, where it was stored. The tires were flat, of course, so he had to find the pump and inflate them. After all this effort, the old man was breathing hard, but the thought of the fish he was going to bring home made him jubilant. His wife was every bit as elated as he as she watched him bustling about.

"I'm leaving," he called as he pushed the bicycle out the door.

"Hurry back," she said. "If you can manage to buy a fish, that'll be just grand."

Kuai Shifu turned out of the small lane onto Cockcrow Temple Road, which led all the way to the south gate of People's Park and was always crowded. Accustomed as he was to lining up for the bus before daybreak, Kuai Shifu rode his bicycle with a great feeling of freedom and exhilaration. As he wove in and out among the pedestrians, the hoarse sound of the bell was music to his ears. When he turned onto the wider and more congested Beijing Avenue, trucks began whizzing past him one after another as they sped toward Drum Tower Circle. The old man had always dreaded traffic at the circle, so he took a shortcut through a small alley and quickly reached Dongren Street.

It had been a long time since his last visit to the market. In fact, it had been over a year, when his son had come home on leave from the Northeast, and Kuai Shifu had gotten up very early one morning to buy a chicken.

The market on Dongren Street and the Central Market on New Market Square were both well known. The Municipal Revolutionary Committee looked upon them as places of importance, so they were excellently managed and always well stocked with a wide assortment of fish, meat, and vegetables. Although a good many people came from far away to shop there, the Kuais were not among them. Most of the people who patronized these two markets were People's Liberation Army personnel and the servants of families of high-level Party members who lived in the area. They spent their money freely, and Mama Kuai, who had always lived a frugal life, disapproved of their ways.

The first thing Kuai Shifu noticed was that the entire street had been renovated since his last visit. The grounds had been swept clean and the walls had been washed; and the newly posted political slogans were particularly attractive. Whether they were selling soy sauce, pickled vegetables, groceries, brooms, or toilet paper, the shops on both sides of the street looked as though they had all been carefully rearranged. The windows shone, and even the door fronts had been scrubbed until the bricks were bright red.

Kuai Shifu parked his bicycle at the entrance to the marketplace and walked in with his basket. The spotless cement floor had obviously just been washed, so that as he walked, Kuai Shifu looked back guiltily at the footprints his large cotton-padded shoes had made. There weren't many customers in the market, but there were enough so that every stall had some business. All the stall keepers were wearing freshly washed and starched white knee-length aprons, while those selling meat and fish even had white cotton caps on their heads.

Of all the places in the market, Kuai Shifu liked the fish stall the best. The shiny tile counter made the various kinds of fish on display particularly attractive. From a distance, he could see the ribbon-fish and bream that covered the stand. But he could also see that there was a line of people waiting. Just as he was about to get in line, he spotted some other fish on the counter. He stepped forward and saw several large *qing* fish,* all shiny and fresh-looking, laid out in a row.

"Why buy bream when there is *qing* fish?" he thought. Bream has a muddy taste that no amount of seasoning can get rid of.

He saw a stall keeper busily weighing fish, calling out the weights as his free hand clicked the abacus. Another man was squatting in a corner sorting fish from a big wooden box, throwing the large ones into one basket and the small ones into another. Kuai Shifu tried to catch the second man's attention. He called out, "Are these *qing* fish for sale?"

---

*A flat gray freshwater fish, popular in central China for making soup.

The man looked up, frowning at him for some time before answering, "They're out on the stand, so of course they're for sale."

"Then weigh me half a fish!" As he spoke he placed his basket beside the stand, trying to make up his mind which half of the fish he should buy. Mama Kuai had said she wanted some fish soup, and the fish head would make a tastier soup than a chicken! So he'd better buy the top half.

"Give me the top half, with the head."

"Can't sell half a fish," the stall keeper answered, shaking his head as he went back to his sorting. "If you want it, you'll have to take the whole fish!"

The old man hesitated. Buy the whole fish? He looked at the price—sixty-five fen a catty. A whole fish would come to two or three yuan. His hand instinctively moved up to the pocket of his quilted jacket.

"Well?" the man asked, raising his head again. Seeing the look of indecision on Kuai's face, he added coldly, "Each one weighs about four or five catties."

The stall keeper's attitude annoyed Kuai. He patted the top of his jacket where his month's pay, which he'd just received, lay hidden in his inner pocket.

"Okay, go ahead and weigh the whole fish!" he answered briskly.

This caught the man by surprise. Giving Kuai a hard look, he got up slowly and, without saying a word, picked up a large fish and put it on the hook of the steelyard.

"Oh, I'd like that one," Kuai Shifu hastily pointed to a smaller fish.

"What's the matter?" The stall keeper pretended not to understand. Lifting the steelyard higher, he swung the dangling fish in front of his customer's face so that the tail nearly brushed against Kuai's chin.

The old man took a step backward and waved his hand in a conciliatory gesture. "Go ahead and weigh it." He'd better not make a fuss, he decided. He consoled himself with the thought that it was a rare opportunity to get such good fish, even though it meant that he and his wife would have to eat fish for the next three days. Luckily the weather was cold, and the fish would not spoil.

"Sixty-five fen . . . four and a half catties . . . that comes to two yuan, ninety-three fen." The stall keeper blinked and announced the price without bothering to use his abacus.

Kuai quickly took a five-yuan bill from his inner pocket. The man gave him his change and carefully placed the fish in the basket. After another curious look at Kuai Shifu, he went back to sorting fish.

The old man let out a deep sigh, but he picked up his market basket and left the fish stall with a feeling of satisfaction. Those young fellows were right, he thought. This Dongren Street market was quite a place; a person can actually buy a large *qing* fish here. He was sure his wife wouldn't believe her eyes when she saw the size of the fish. Absorbed in his own sense of accomplishment and grinning happily, he didn't notice the curious looks the other customers were giving him. Some of them were even pointing at his basket.

As he passed a vegetable stand, Kuai Shifu's eyes lit up. At the end of February produce was always scarce, and he would never have thought that there could be so many kinds of vegetables on display. In addition to the turnips, carrots, and frozen cabbages that were usually available, there were also tomatoes and cucumbers—things he hadn't seen for a long time. These delicacies were attractively displayed in separate little baskets placed at the most conspicuous spots in the stand. He looked at the price of the tomatoes—fifty fen a catty. He shook his head. They were intentionally priced out of the common people's reach, he thought. In the summer they were only five fen a catty. There was no price on the cucumbers, but since his wife had always been fond of them, he decided to get one, whatever the cost, just so she could eat some fresh vegetables. After being ill for several days, she'd enjoy the taste of something different.

"How much are the cucumbers?" he asked a woman vendor.

"The cucumbers aren't for sale!" she answered bluntly, her eyes fixed on the fish in his basket.

The old man was disappointed, but since there was nothing he could do, he looked around to see what he could get to cook with the fish head.

"Hurry! Hurry! There are people in line behind you!" The woman gestured impatiently with the steelyard, sending the lead weight and bronze plate clanging against each other.

Under this pressure, Kuai Shifu lost his composure and couldn't make up his mind. All of a sudden he remembered that they might be out of ginger at home. "Give me a half a catty of tender ginger." Then he spotted a small basket of bamboo shoots in a corner. He knew that bamboo shoots were expensive, but they'd be delicious cooked with the fish head. He thought of how frugal his wife had been through the years, and decided that she deserved at least one good meal now that she was ill. Bamboo shoots cooked with the fish head—he hadn't indulged in such luxury in years. "Give me two bamboo shoots." This time he didn't even bother to ask the price.

"Sixty-five fen a catty," the woman announced. She emptied the ginger into his basket and went over to weigh the bamboo shoots.

After paying for the vegetables, Kuai Shifu picked up the market basket. Feeling its weight, he decided not to buy anything else, but to go straight home and cook the fish. Countless varieties of dishes were displayed in the glass showcases on the prepared food counter, but he gave them only a cursory glance as he hurried toward the main entrance.

More people were coming to shop now. Housewives, laborers coming from work, cadremen, and soldiers in neat uniforms were pouring into the market. He walked over to the place where he had parked his bicycle, which was now just one among many.

"Comrade, is there any more of that fish left?" A man who brushed by him turned back to ask anxiously.

"Yes!" he assured the man enthusiastically. "Hurry, there are still several . . ." Before he'd finished speaking, a housewife carrying a basket hurried up to him and broke in, "Comrade, how much is this fish selling for? Is there a long line?"

"No need to stand in line. It's sixty-five fen a catty."

After all the attention his market basket had attracted, Kuai Shifu took another look at the large *qing* fish. With its clear bulging eyes and bright scales, it was impressive looking indeed. The old man's heart was filled with joy.

He carefully hung the market basket on the handlebar of his bicycle. Because of the crowd, he had to push the bicycle out to Dongren Street. But when he was about to get on his bicycle, someone tapped him on the shoulder.

"Hey, comrade, take that fish back."

The old man lowered his right leg to the ground and turned

to see a middle-aged man with small protruding eyes. From his manner and dress, the old man could tell he was a cadre member.

"What did you say?" He thought the man had mistaken him for someone else.

"That fish isn't for sale," the man said in a low voice, trying to be patient. "Take it back to the cashier's office immediately, and they'll refund you what you paid for it."

"What?" Kuai raised his voice. "Not for sale? Damn it! Then why the hell didn't they say so in the first place? Now you want to snatch it away when it's about to be dropped in the pot!"

At the old man's curses the cadreman's face hardened and he glared at Kuai.

"If they're all sold out, what'll be left to show the foreign visitors when they arrive?"

Kuai Shifu wanted to say something more to give vent to his grievance, but when he heard the words "foreign visitors" he stopped short. The issue was closed. He gulped, then blinked his eyes in stony silence.

The cadreman, seeing that Kuai was not responding, demanded, "What unit do you belong to?"

His insolent tone of voice angered Kuai Shifu, who blurted out, "Nanjing Dockyard, ironworker for thirty years!" To save himself from further questioning, he gave his type of work and the length of time he had served.

The cadreman softened when he heard that Kuai was an old worker. "Never mind," he said, nodding his head. "You didn't know. Just take the fish back, and the cashier's office will . . ."

"If you want the fish," the old man broke in, "you take it! I'm not going to!"

He recalled the hard looks the man at the fish stall had given him. Now if he were to take the fish back, not only the stall keeper but all the people in the market would stare at him.

A crowd had gathered by this time, looking curiously at the two men. The cadreman was afraid the matter might get out of hand, so he backed down. "I'll take it back for you," he said, "Wait here. I'll bring the money back right away."

Without waiting for an answer, he thrust his hand into the basket and grabbed the fish. With everyone's eyes riveted on him, he walked into the market, holding the fish by the gills.

Kuai Shifu looked on helplessly as the fish, its huge tail swinging back and forth, disappeared into the distance. He looked into the basket again. It was empty except for a few pieces of ginger root and two withered bamboo shoots. He could go back and try to buy a bream, but it would probably be all sold out by now. Then as he thought of the long lines, his legs felt weak.

What would he say to Mama Kuai when he got home? That was the most difficult part. She'd be even more disappointed if she found out just how close she'd come to feasting on that fish. It would probably be best to tell her a lie. In all their years of marriage, Kuai had never lied to his wife.

As he stood there, dazed, a bystander came up and said to him, "You don't seem to know the ropes, do you? Before the foreign visitors have come to look, they won't sell any of the good things. We're all waiting until the foreigners have come and gone before we try to buy any of the specials."

"You can buy them before the foreign visitors arrive," someone said sarcastically with a knowing air. "The only trouble is that you have to take them back. Last time, when Prince Sihanouk came to Nanjing, they even brought in turkeys from somewhere. One of my neighbors, who'd never seen a turkey, bought one out of curiosity. But he only got it as far as the rear gate before it was sent back. They said they started with five turkeys, and after two days of brisk sales, there were still five turkeys left!"

Kuai Shifu couldn't bear to listen any longer. He turned abruptly, and with a backward kick of his right leg, mounted his bicycle.

"Comrade, he hasn't given you back your money!"

"Tell him to give it to the foreign visitors!"

Geng Er
in Beijing

I

Although closing early on Saturdays was not stipulated anywhere, by tacit understanding everyone began wrapping things up soon after three, and promptly at four they left the office, one after the other. For Geng Er this day was like all others: Precisely at four o'clock he walked out of the Research Institute of Mechanics, climbed onto his old English racing bike, and, without first stopping off at his dormitory, rode out through the gate of the Academy of Sciences and headed straight for the city. In the western suburbs of Beijing in early November the sky is clear and the air is crisp, cool without being cold. Geng Er shifted into third gear. Whipping along like the wind and chasing after his own shadow with the afternoon sun at his back, he felt elated, putting all the tedium and monotony of the past week out of his mind.

The traffic grew more congested after he passed through the West Gate area, forcing him to slow down. But since he was so familiar with this stretch of road that he could have negotiated it with his eyes closed, he soon arrived at the northern gate of the East Wind Market at Wangfujing. As he parked his bicycle at the stand he saw a line of people stretched all the way to the parking lot waiting for numbers. A bad sign, he thought; he wouldn't have a chance of getting a number. But in spite of that, he ran over and got on the end of the line. What everyone was eagerly awaiting were the hot pots served by a specialty restaurant. Each day only forty pots were prepared and forty numbers distributed. The first twenty were served from five-thirty to seven o'clock, and the other half from seven on. Since there simply were not enough to go around, people who had a special liking for the mutton hot pot, which was the restaurant's specialty, sometimes started lining up at the foot of the stairs at three in the afternoon.

It was as Geng Er had anticipated. Before long there was a stir in front of the line as the last number was given out, and the people began to disperse, not without some grumbling. Geng Er drew close to the foot of the stairs and waited patiently for those who had been given the last twenty numbers to clear away.

"Mr. Geng!"

Lao Lu, the employee responsible for parceling out the numbers, was waving to him from the top of the stairs. Geng Er was so pleased he dashed up the stairs, two and three steps at a time. Lao Lu unobtrusively placed a small piece of greasy cardboard in his hand. He looked gratefully at Lao Lu, walked into the restaurant, and found a seat by the window.

He placed the ticket on the table in front of him. He felt a little guilty when he saw that it was number eleven. Only that morning during the political study session, besides the criticisms of Lin Biao and Confucius, the discussion had touched on ways of stopping the evil practice of getting things through the back door. Geng Er was the last one to speak, making an impassioned statement. One of his colleagues was taking minutes, and tried frantically to get it down completely. But did he truly feel guilty? A helpless shrug was his only answer. Everyone shouted and carried on about closing off back doors, yet in private his colleagues invariably discussed how they could find such back doors for themselves. Since Geng Er lived all alone and his needs were few, he had managed to refrain from this evil practice.

Naturally, eating mutton hot pot was an exception.

This particular back door had been opened to him quite naturally. Ever since the renovation of the East Wind Market and the opening of this restaurant, Geng Er had been a regular customer. Nearly every week, on Saturday or Sunday, he would have a meal of mutton hot pot, and so he had become friendly with Lao Lu. The old Beijing Muslim was about ten years older than Geng Er. His hair was nearly all gray, but his teeth were still white and even, and he cordially flashed them for the benefit of his customers. Neither man knew the other's full name, and at first they had simply called each other Lao Lu and Lao Geng. When Lu learned that Geng Er worked in the Academy of Sciences, he became very respectful and began calling him Mr. Geng. This filled Geng Er with regret, but it was too late to do anything about it. He was glad he hadn't told him that he was a returned overseas scholar who had lived in America for twenty years. That would have made matters even worse.

Lao Lu knew that Geng Er was a bachelor and could appreciate his coming into the city from such a distance in order to eat a meal. So on weekends Lu often took it upon himself to hold back one of the numbers for Geng Er. Such consideration was not easy to come by, so Geng Er came even more often.

A young waiter brought a bowl and a pair of chopsticks to his table, and Geng Er ordered several dishes of sliced beef and mutton, plus some bean-flour noodles, cabbage, and some thin baked wheat cakes. When the waiter had added up the check, Geng Er handed him a bill and his ration card, and then put the receipt under his bowl. While the people around him were busily ordering food and paying their checks, he reached into the pocket of his Mao jacket and took out a small vial of alcohol and two wads of cotton. Holding his chopsticks under the table, he wiped them off with the cotton balls, then did the same with his bowl.

Ever since several of his colleagues had come down with hepatitis, supposedly from eating in restaurants, he had been on the alert. One of his colleagues had told him about this method of disinfecting eating utensils, but he always felt a bit guilty about it and was especially afraid that Lao Lu might see him.

"Is there anyone else at this table?" a neatly dressed old man asked Geng Er with a smile. He shook his head, and surreptitiously dropped the cotton balls on the floor. The old man placed his numbered ticket on the table, removed his wool cap and hung it on the wall along with his cane, then leisurely sat down opposite Geng Er. I must took like a doddering old man myself, Geng Er thought as he smothered a sigh, since only old people in their seventies and eighties are willing to share a table with me. The thought reminded him of his own age. For a moment he was unable to say just exactly *how* old he was; then he quietly calculated to himself: 1974, 1925 . . . he was precisely forty-nine. Ah, forty-nine! The thought was like a gulp of ice water that left a cold track all the way to the bottom of his heart. The number nine was some sort of milestone in his life: at twenty-nine he'd received his Ph.D., at thirty-nine he'd returned to China, and now he was forty-nine. Ten years already! He was single and alone when he returned, and he was still single and alone.

"Is something wrong?" the old man asked solicitously. His hair was white, his face kindly, his expression refined yet friendly.

"No, it's nothing . . ." Geng Er knew he'd forgotten himself and had somehow betrayed his inner feelings, and now he felt embarrassed.

"Nice weather we're having; just the time to be eating mutton hot pot," the old man said, tactfully changing the subject.

Just then Lao Lu appeared with a large round tray. Geng Er welcomed his presence and called out warmly, "Lao Lu, how's everything these days?"

"Just fine, just fine!" Lao Lu answered crisply. He put down the tray, removed from it eight or nine dishes of sliced meat and vegetables, and laid them out on the table in front of Geng Er.

"Any news from your son?"

"Still the same!" Lao Lu said with a sigh. "I've always said that the boy was born without any luck, but his mother wouldn't believe it. See for yourself. He and his classmates were sent to resettle in Inner Mongolia, and all those who are sons and daughters of cadre members have been recalled and admitted to universities. A fellow who joined his group only last year is now studying English at the Institute of Foreign Languages. I asked him why he couldn't be more like that Zhang Tiesheng, who dashed off an anti-establishment letter and had himself sent to Liaoning Agricultural College."

Lao Lu was so concerned with giving vent to his feelings that he gave no thought to being overheard. But his complaint was a common one and attracted no attention.

"Well, he's still young. There'll be other opportunities," Geng Er said in an attempt to console him.

"He's already twenty-five and his old man still has to send him food and clothing. And if his mother wants to see him, the only way he can get home is for us to send him travel money."

Having unburdened himself, Lao Lu abruptly bent over and whispered to Geng Er, "How about you? Any good news to report?"

Geng Er shook his head. Lao Lu gave him a comforting pat on the shoulder, then picked up the other man's ticket and walked away.

Geng Er and the old man picked up their bowls and went over to get the sauces and spices, and by the time they returned, the old man's dishes had been placed on the table. The waiter threw the change on the table and walked away.

"Hey, comrade, I still have a plate of bean-flour noodles coming." The old man tried to catch the attention of his waiter, but he kept walking, as if he were deaf.

"What an attitude!" The old man shook his head and smiled wryly as he sat down with an air of resignation.

"Forget it, comrade," Geng Er said as he pushed his own bowl of noodles over. "I have more here than I need."

Just as the old man was about to push it back, Lao Lu walked up with Geng Er's hot pot. As he lifted the lid, the air was filled with steam.

"Thank you. Thank you very much!" Geng Er said appreciatively.

The old man took the opportunity to tell the old waiter about the bean-flour noodles.

"Okay, okay! I'll bring some right away," Lao Lu promised as he took a white towel from his shoulder and mopped his brow. Then he turned to Geng Er. "Eat it while it's hot. Would you like me to get you a glass of Bamboo Green liquor?"

"No need for that, Lao Lu, I'll get it myself."

Geng Er jumped to his feet. Getting liquor for the customers wasn't the waiters' job, and Lao Lu, especially, was so busy his face was covered with sweat. By this time all the tables were filled with customers, some of whom were getting impatient and were waving and shouting for their hot pots.

"The Anti–Lin Biao, Anti-Confucius campaign ought to be winding down now, Mr. Geng," the old waiter whispered into his ear as he accompanied him over to the liquor counter. "We're now in a period of policy implementation, so you ought to take advantage of the relaxed atmosphere to have one of your colleagues introduce you to a prospective wife."

Geng Er said nothing. He simply shook his head and smiled as Lao Lu gave him another consoling pat on the shoulder and walked toward the kitchen.

What a warm friend! Geng Er was genuinely moved. But such things are more easily said than done. As a matter of fact, getting him married was a matter of considerable interest in his office. His chief and his colleagues had expressed their concern, but where was a man of his years to find a suitable spouse? Back in 1968 a young colleague—a conspicuous member of the rebel faction—had said to him, "If you hadn't studied in America, a man of your caliber would long since have had a family!"

He was right on the mark. In those days the status of repatriated Chinese was quite low, especially those who came from America. In the eyes of the rebels, they were either secret agents or incorrigible capitalists. Geng Er knew that behind his back his colleagues already considered him the "major problem case" in the institute.

Geng Er brought two glasses of liquor back to the table, then raised his chopsticks to invite the old man to share his meal with him. "You needn't stand on ceremony; go ahead and eat," the old man said, acknowledging this polite gesture.

Just then the other hot pot arrived, and the old man went to the wine counter and bought a large glass of red grape wine. With great ceremony he raised his glass and toasted Geng Er, who returned the toast. As Geng Er closed his eyes and savored the sweet taste of the liquor, he thought of Xiao Qing, for it was she who had introduced him to this delicious liquor.

"So you like Bamboo Green," the old man remarked as he put down his own glass. "I can't drink it; it's even more potent than sorghum liquor."

"It doesn't bother me," Geng Er replied. "It's sweet, but it has a slight medicinal taste. A friend of mine introduced me to it with mutton hot pot, and I just got used to it. I always have it with mutton hot pot."

"Oh, so that's how it is." The old man nodded, seeming to understand. "I used to like only Shaoxing rice wine myself, and my wife liked grape wine. But ever since she passed away I've taken to drinking grape wine."

"Is that so?" said Geng Er sympathetically.

Xiao Qing, he thought, lives in Beijing, but as far as he was concerned, she might as well not exist. He could almost see her standing before him, with her dark, moist eyes and her long braids. The liquor suddenly seemed to freeze into beads of ice, cold and hard, beating relentlessly against his heart. After the interminable Cultural Revolution had passed, the memories of his aborted love affair faded into the past, but he was left with a taste very much like that of Bamboo Green—sweet with a trace of bitterness.

He remembered well his first drink of Bamboo Green, at a restaurant in the western part of the city. Xiao Qing had received her 1965 year-end bonus and invited him to eat mutton hot pot in celebration of the Lunar New Year.

"If you don't learn to appreciate mutton hot pot you might as well not live in Beijing," she said. "Don't be fooled by the crowds in restaurants that specialize in Beijing duck. They are actually for visitors from the provinces. Old-time Beijing people don't go in for it much."

Geng Er had been born and raised in Shanghai, and in his home they never ate mutton. During his years in America he disliked the smell of stewed lamb. But he readily fell in with Xiao Qing's suggestion and was surprised to find how delicious it was. He was intrigued by the way it was prepared and served; it was much better than roast duck, all oozing with fat.

The Chinese like to talk about "predestination," and although Geng Er was no longer a believer, he hadn't doubted it at all when he first met Xiao Qing. How else could he explain his finding her in a city as big as Beijing? If he hadn't ventured out on his bicycle in the bitter cold weather following the snows in early 1965 to browse through bookstores, wouldn't he have missed the chance of meeting her? He was grateful also to the New China Bookstore for displaying its dictionaries on a high shelf, for that was the stroke of luck that led to a soft, melodious voice asking him, "Would you mind handing me a copy of the *Concise English–Chinese Dictionary?*"

He turned in the direction of the voice, and there she was. Those eyes of hers, shielded by long lashes, were so bright and clear they reminded him of a glacial lake in the Rockies he'd visited in the United States—so bright it had made him dizzy and so still it had seemed removed from this world.

"Are you a student?" It was the only thing he could think to ask as he handed her the book; he was afraid he might never again see those star-like eyes of hers.

"No, I'm a worker at the Third Textile Mill," she said with candor and pride.

She then told him that the workers were encouraged to study a foreign language, and that she had signed up for the English class. Discovering that she was a local girl, Geng Er asked her where he could find second-hand bookstores. She told him that the best one was located in the Bridge of Heaven district, an amusement center in southern Beijing, and, seeing that he was unfamiliar with the city, she decided to accompany him there. Since she'd also come by bicycle, they rode together to the Bridge of Heaven.

"Xiao Qing." He could not keep from whispering her name now as he took a sip of liquor.

All twenty of the hot pots in the restaurant were now open, and clouds of steam filled the room. Glasses and plates covered the tables, and there was lively conversation everywhere. Geng Er noticed that the old man's glass was empty and that his once pale face was now suffused with a red glow; he was at the moment unbuttoning his wool overcoat with slightly trembling hands and breathing through his mouth.

The image of Xiao Qing's father and the hearty way he drank popped into Geng Er's head. The first time he called on her family, the father had asked him to stay for dinner and sent her younger brother out to buy some prepared food. Then he brought out a bottle of Bamboo Green that he'd been hoarding for more than six months. The father would tilt his head back to allow each swallow to course down his throat. Then he'd reach out with his chopsticks, pick up three slices of tripe, and put them in his mouth. So natural, so completely without affectation. He told Geng Er a great many things about life in Beijing before Liberation, and recalled his experiences as a porter at the railroad station. Warmed by the liquor, he even removed his overcoat and fanned himself with a folded newspaper. He was feeling quite merry by the time they finished the bottle. He warmly patted Geng Er on the back and began to sing in a loud voice—fashionable revolutionary songs as well as some obscure melodies.

What a delightful old man! And Xiao Qing was just like him.

Geng Er had never met a girl who was so frank and open, so artless—a simple, sincere, and completely natural girl. Except for her large eyes and long lashes, she looked nothing like the girl of his dreams: her skin was not fair, she was not tall, and she was not a college student. What's more, she was nineteen years younger than he. And yet she exerted a mysterious force upon him, drawing him to her like a magnet and holding him tightly against her. From the moment of their first meeting, Geng Er no longer felt rootless and alone, as he had during all his years as a drifter in a strange land. When he was with her not only was he indescribably happy but he also felt safe and secure. With the release of all his suppressed emotions, there was no need to struggle to keep up appearances. He felt he had reverted to the innocence of childhood. Xiao Qing loved to laugh, and her laugh was so cheerful, so bright, and so warm that it brought spring and sunshine wherever she went.

After parting at the Bridge of Heaven he went at once to a store and bought himself a second-hand Shanghai bicycle in good condition. Then he returned to his dormitory and put away his English racer. How flashy and conspicuous his new foreign bicycle had appeared alongside her old domestic bicycle! Soon after their first meeting Xiao Qing discovered that he'd studied abroad, but she didn't hold that against him at all, unlike so many of his colleagues who called him "The Yankee" behind his back, making him feel like a steer that has been branded with an indelible mark.

Xiao Qing was a model worker of New China. She was filled with pride and dignity but was also capable of maintaining an attitude toward foreign things that was neither superior nor obsequious. In this she differed from many of Geng Er's younger colleagues at the institute, who generally disparaged anything and everything foreign on principle, but on occasion betrayed a blind admiration for such things. In point of fact, she was full of curiosity for anything new. On those occasions when Geng Er mentioned the history of some foreign nation or some wonder of nature he had seen, she listened with wide-eyed curiosity and rapt attention. Sometimes she asked him endless questions, wanting desperately to get to the bottom of everything. She worked even harder at her English, now that Geng Er was her teacher. In the summer of that year the two of them often went to the rear hill of the Summer Palace to study. It was much quieter there among the trees than on the shores of Kunming Lake, which attracted most of the tourists.

Geng Er never tried to conceal his feelings, though he never expressed them in words either, for fear that the pressure on Xiao Qing would be too great. At the time she was only twenty years old, a whole generation younger than he, and he knew that it was up to him to control himself. He would have to proceed slowly and not force himself on her. His love could not be like the white heat of the noonday sun, its rays shining everywhere; instead he had to pattern himself after the setting sun, warm without scorching. But the tenderness and affection in the depths of his heart were like the lava in an underground volcano, which seethed and flowed in search of the opportunity to explode to the surface. Xiao Qing was somewhat hesitant at first—Geng Er assumed that she was troubled by the differences between them in nearly every respect—but as summer approached she gradually warmed to him, even taking it upon herself to change her day off at the mill to Sunday so they could be together. When she saw a co-worker with whom she was friendly she would cheerfully call out to her and then introduce Geng Er.

"Mr. Geng, here, have some candy." Lao Lu broke in on his thoughts.

"What's the happy occasion?" Geng Er asked as he laid down his chopsticks and picked up the three pieces of soft candy Lao Lu had placed in front of him.

"Our chief cook got married today and treated us all." Lao Lu had a big grin on his face, as though he himself were getting married. He had brought a pot of hot water to refill the two hot pots on the table. "Don't forget, now, I expect to be repaid three-fold when you pass out your own wedding candy." With that, he turned to pour hot water at another table.

"You can count on it," Geng Er assured him as he put the candy in his pocket.

Will that day ever come? he asked himself. In his youth he had assumed it would, and he'd eagerly looked forward to it.

He raised his glass again and gazed at it absent-mindedly. What a striking green color and what a fragrant bouquet! But how could it ever compare with the beauty of Xiao Qing's face and her intoxicating scent?

On a holiday in the autumn of 1965 Geng Er and Xiao Qing went to Fragrant Mountain to enjoy the maple leaves. Since it was early in the season, the leaves at the base of the mountain hadn't turned yet, and they took a walk up the mountain to seek the brighter colors. Xiao Qing was wearing a new lined jacket, and her shiny hair was neatly braided and tied at the ends with red silk. As she walked those two enchanting silk bands danced atop her shoulders. Halfway up the mountain they came across a clump of maple leaves that had turned red and stopped to admire them. Xiao Qing picked a red leaf and handed it to him. Her lips were brighter than the leaf, and Geng Er could not keep from taking her face in his hands and gently kissing her. She did not try to resist him, though she blushed a deep crimson and kept her eyes lowered for a long time.

Ah, those days were beautiful beyond imagining. Geng Er was walking on air. His heart was so full of love he could not have expressed it if he'd had an eternity. It was like a stream that has been awakened from its winter sleep by a night of spring rain, suddenly so swollen it threatens to overflow its banks.

At forty, love had come to him late, but it had come nonetheless. He had known other women, but never had he been so swept off his feet. There had been few Chinese girls around during his first years in America, and since things in short supply are always cherished, those young women had been disdainful of Chinese men and criticized their every flaw. And so Geng Er decided to remove himself from the competition. As for American girls, they were ardent and unrestrained, and he found many who were responsive. He was tempted several times, but the thought that he would someday return to his own country made him unwilling to consider marriage. Thinking back to those austere times, those years of deprivation that finally led to a better life, Geng Er realized that there hadn't been a single girl who could match the innocence, sincerity, and desirability of Xiao Qing.

Not only was he in love with her, he was enchanted by her family as well. It was on the Sunday following their excursion to Fragrant Mountain that she first invited him to her home. Her parents were such kind old people that they immediately gained his complete respect and admiration. Old Mr. Xue had spent half his life as a porter, but after Liberation he was among the first batch of workers admitted to the textile mill that had been built in Beijing. He had just retired that year. His wife had given birth to seven children, but only the last three had grown to adulthood: one son was serving in the army; their daughter was honored every year as a model worker; and the youngest, also a son, was about to graduate from middle school. And so the old couple was perfectly content and full of gratitude to the Communist Party. On the wall beside their brick bed hung several newspaper photographs of Liu Shaoqi, Premier Zhou, and Chairman Mao.

On the day of the visit they had been preparing the filled dumplings called *jiaozi*, and although Geng Er could not cook at all, during his years in America he had learned how to make *jiaozi* wraps. So he rolled up his sleeves and set to work. He worked quickly, making each wrap paper-thin. The old couple was astounded and showered him with praise. He had come with misgivings, afraid that Xiao Qing's parents would be critical of his background, but they soon put him at ease and treated him fondly, as they would their own son. Old Mr. Xue even asked him to stay to share his bottle, and if it hadn't been for Xiao Qing's presence, Geng Er would have let himself get roaring drunk that night. After dinner Xiao Qing saw him out and walked hand in hand with him past two bus stops before reluctantly letting him get on a bus.

In his excitement he lay awake all that night, wondering when to propose to her and trying to visualize how blissful their married life would be. He had only recently returned to China; filled with hope for the future, he was confident that he could find his niche in the new society. He had spent twenty-one years in school and then taught for ten years; this and the fact that his parents had also been teachers convinced him that he was a classic example of a petty bourgeois intellectual. A union with Xiao Qing, who came from a long line of workers, would mean not only a complete turnaround in his thoughts, but also that his children would inherit the noble blood of the working class. What could be more meaningful than that?

The next day Geng Er skipped supper and rode his bicycle right from work to a department store where he spent the equivalent of three months' salary on an Omega watch as an engagement gift for Xiao Qing. He yearned to buy her all the beautiful things that were on display, but when he recalled her temperament, he just sighed. Although she had to contribute a large portion of her monthly salary of forty-two yuan to the support of her family, with high hopes and determination she had begun a savings plan so that in two years she would be able to buy a wristwatch made in Shanghai. She did not like Geng Er to spend a lot of money on her, and sometimes insisted on treating him. Being used to the custom of giving flowers and gifts as a means of courting, Geng Er was impressed by her independence and staunch self-respect, and he loved and admired her all the more for it. This girl of New China, ardent and yet solemn, gentle and yet strong, bewitched him no end.

It was in the midst of this, the greatest happiness he had ever known, that the Great Cultural Revolution was ushered in. Never having been through a political campaign, Geng Er welcomed it enthusiastically; once it has passed, he thought, he and Xiao Qing could be married. In the spring of 1966 she put in a verbal request at the textile mill and was told by her superiors that the matter could be taken care of after the campaign had run its course. But as the campaign spread and widened they had few opportunities to meet. With the coming of summer Red Guards filled the streets, Xiao Qing's younger brother among them, and then Xiao Qing suggested that she and Geng Er not be seen together because other people were "talking about them." This perplexed and pained him a great deal, for he never dreamed that Xiao Qing, who was so strong and independent, would be afraid of what other people said. But the most severe blow came when he returned from an assignment to find that she had sent back the wristwatch.

Suddenly a hush fell over the restaurant as everyone turned toward the head of the stairs. Geng Er put down his empty glass and followed the others' glances. Two men dressed like cadre members were accompanying two other Chinese men in Western suits up to the next floor.

"Foreign visitors," the old man at his table said casually.

"Overseas Chinese," a young man at the next table spat out hatefully.

"I hear that the upper floor is reserved for foreigners," the old man said as he turned back to face Geng Er.

"That's right," said Geng Er. "Everything's the same, except that they eat in more comfortable surroundings."

"Is that so?" the old man replied, staring at Geng Er.

Geng Er said nothing as he busily added some noodles and cabbage to the pot. He did not want to disclose the fact that two weeks earlier he too had been up there, thanks to an old school friend from the University of Chicago, Professor Li. In the other man's wake he had climbed to the spacious, elegantly appointed upper level. The four men in their party had had a large room and several smiling waiters all to themselves.

"This is one of those unavoidable class problems during the transitional stage of a socialist society," the young man at the next table was saying sarcastically. "Once Communism becomes a reality the upper floor will be abolished and everyone will stand in line for tickets and eat with the crowd downstairs."

"Here's hoping that Communism will be here soon!" His associate—also a young man—raised his beer glass.

Geng Er exchanged glances with the old man, then lowered his head and took a bite of his wheat cake.

The thought of his schoolmate filled him with mixed emotions. In America their political views had been worlds apart, and their arguments had often ended in angry partings. But this time when they met they had been very cordial to one another. When Professor Li discovered that Geng Er was still a bachelor, he slapped him on the back and asked in disbelief,

"What? Still unattached after all these years?" Geng Er just smiled and said nothing.

"You know, Lao Geng, you're not getting any younger. You shouldn't be too particular," said his old friend.

Geng Er could only smile wryly and change the subject. He didn't want to tell his friend that the status of the intellectuals had plummeted since the Cultural Revolution, especially since the fall of 1968, when Chairman Mao had directed that all intellectuals be reeducated by the workers, peasants, and soldiers. The intellectuals had to bow their heads and submit meekly to reeducation, and they became outcasts in the new society. So how could he be particular in choosing a mate? It was commendable that his old schoolmate, who had long since become an American citizen, had come back to China to celebrate China's National Day, and Geng Er did not want to dampen his enthusiasm. Besides, since he now took pride in his leftist leanings, he was both unable and unwilling to accept certain facts.

"Reeducation"—as he dwelled on the word, a coldness gripped him. For the past couple of years it was seldom used, but every time he heard it his heart sank, just as it had when he first heard that Xiao Qing had become a member of the Workers' Corps for the Propagation of the Thought of Mao Zedong (shortened to Workers' Propaganda Corps). One day toward the end of 1968 Geng Er rode his bicycle to a spot beyond Chaoyang Gate—even though his love had miscarried because of the Cultural Revolution, he often came there—and ran into Xiao Qing's younger brother. At one time he'd been a proud and overbearing Red Guard leader, but his prestige had evidently waned considerably. Quite unexpectedly it was he who called out to Geng Er. Geng Er first inquired after the boy's parents, then inevitably about Xiao Qing.

"My sister is a member of the Workers' Propaganda Corps!" the boy stated proudly. "She no longer lives at home. Her section has been assigned to the Beijing Technology University and she's the assistant section leader."

Geng Er regretted that he believed in no religion, for he wished he could pray to someone that Xiao Qing not be assigned to the Academy of Sciences. From that time on, whenever he came across a haughty member of the Workers' Propaganda Corps in the Academy, he immediately thought of Xiao Qing, and his heart throbbed.

There is nothing more painful than to be reminded of one's secret sorrow. Unhappily for Geng Er, such reminders came often. The week before was a case in point: After a joyful excursion to the motherland's scenic highlights, Professor Li invited Geng Er to eat at the hotel restaurant. Since it was Professor Li's last night in Beijing, the two men talked far into the night, reminiscing about old times, and the subject of Geng Er's marriage was raised again.

"Lao Geng, you really ought to take my advice," Professor Li said hesitatingly, hoping to avoid any misunderstanding. "A woman doesn't have to be a college graduate to be a good wife. As I understand it, the standard of education is quite high throughout the country. The workers here in Beijing are nice. Oh, yes, the day before yesterday I toured the Third Textile Mill and I saw quite a few pretty young girls there."

Maybe it was because he'd drunk too much Maotai liquor, or maybe he wanted to see if he could face up to his unhappy love affair, but whatever the reason, Geng Er confided in his friend. His old schoolmate listened to the story and was both surprised and sympathetic.

"Is she married now?"

Geng Er shook his head. "I don't know." Although he'd never made inquiries, he was pretty sure she wasn't married. Twice in the past two years he'd caught a glimpse of her, and on both occasions she'd been alone.

"I think you should go see her right away," Professor Li said earnestly. "If she isn't married yet, there's still hope. Isn't there supposed to be a positive attitude toward the intellectuals these days? Who ever heard of a person being ineligible for marriage just because he's a high-level intellectual? Since the working class is supposed to assume leadership in everything, all the more reason for them to marry intellectuals. That way they can facilitate their reeducation!"

His friend clapped his hands and roared with laughter at his own witticism. Geng Er laughed along with him, but there was no laughter in his heart. He was thinking of that day in 1971 when he'd seen her near Tiananmen Square—walking alone across the Bridge of Golden Waters, her head held high, her hair still in braids, but her face serious and her eyes fixed straight ahead. In his excitement, he had barely been able to hold his bicycle steady, and it had taken all his will power to keep from calling out to her. Suddenly drained of his strength, he had pedaled weakly across the square. How he had longed to hold her hands and speak intimately to her, to gaze at length into her eyes, which shone like two meteors on a wintry night. But his courage had left him.

"I understand that this earth-shaking Cultural Revolution has changed a great many people, and that everything has taken on a new look," Professor Li said. "It seems you've changed a great deal yourself."

Geng Er nodded in agreement.

"For better or worse?"

"That depends on your definition of what's good and what's bad," Geng Er answered with a smile.

"You're always so mysterious with me. But let's get back to the matter at hand. I'll be seeing a certain high official tomorrow; would you like me to discuss your problem with him?"

"No, no!" Geng Er shouted.

My God! His heart cried out against sending someone to Xiao Qing, who "held the reins of leadership," recommending that in response to the policy toward intellectuals, she should marry So-and-so.

Shaking his head spiritedly, he said resolutely, "I've gotten used to living alone and I no longer think about getting married."

"Then you must have devoted all your energy to your work. You must have published quite a few papers over the past few years."

Geng Er smiled as he shook his head again. "We place importance only on practical work at the Academy, not on publishing; our emphasis is on cooperative ventures, not individual projects."

How could he tell his friend that he had in fact changed his field, that the program at the institute was constantly shifting to suit the needs of the revolution? In the final analysis, I'm a Chinese, he told himself: how I feel is my own business, but defending the national image is a moral obligation. This most likely is the dialectical application of Mao's "one divides into two" theory.

It was getting late, and Geng Er got up to leave, but his old schoolmate was loath to say goodbye and walked him to the door of the hotel, switching to English as he said to him, "Lao Geng, is there anything you'd like me to do for you?"

After a moment's thought, Geng Er smiled and answered, "Yes, there is. Come back often, so I can go along with you to restaurants reserved for foreign visitors. That would give me more pleasure than anything else."

More pleasure than anything else!

"Hm?" The old man across the table was staring at him. "What were you saying?"

Geng Er realized that he'd forgotten himself again, but he was beginning to feel the effects of the liquor, so he answered without embarrassment, "I was saying that eating mutton hot pot gives me more pleasure than anything else."

"I agree, I agree completely," the old man said, nodding vigorously.

The two of them picked up pieces of mutton with their chopsticks and ate with gusto.

II

A few days before the Lunar New Year's holidays some of Geng Er's unmarried colleagues began leaving Beijing to join their families, and those who remained did not feel much like working. On the final day of the old year they managed to drag through the morning, and not long after lunch they too left. Alone in the deserted institute, Geng Er had no desire to stick around, so he left before three o'clock and went home to his dormitory.

The Lunar New Year is still the most important Chinese festival, with a tradition of thousands of years. Even the preparation of food is more elaborate than that of the National Day celebrations. Geng Er could hear the other people in the dormitory chopping and mincing meat to make the filling for *jiaozi;* in fact the same sound had awakened him early that morning.

He removed his hat and gloves and took his customary turn through the bedroom and the living room. His apartment was even quieter and more deserted than the institute. Ten years earlier, when he'd moved into the two-room apartment, he'd found it too small and crowded, but the longer he lived there, the bigger and emptier it seemed. He often secretly congratulated himself, for in Beijing it was rare indeed for a single person to have a two-room place with room to walk around in.

He felt tired, so he headed for the kitchen to make a cup of coffee to drive out the cold and pick him up a bit. Over the last couple of years he had stopped drinking coffee in the afternoon, for fear it would keep him awake at night, but this was New Year's eve and he seized upon the excuse.

Geng Er had given Wang Dasao,* his housekeeper, a week off over the holidays. He didn't feel any need to straighten up the place—it would be strange indeed if anyone came to see him—and so his bed was in disarray, looking as though he had just gotten out of it. He could not abide the job of washing his own clothes, so he simply didn't change his shirt; if he had, there'd be a pile of dirty clothes awaiting Wang Dasao's return. That could be interpreted as exploiting her labor, despite the fact that as she was leaving she repeatedly told him—almost begged him—to leave his clothes for her to wash when she returned.

---

*Literally "elder sister-in-law," Dasao is used here as a courtesy title.

"I'm a bachelor, through and through," he thought aloud as he entered the kitchen.

There was a mountain of dirty dishes in the sink, and he would have to wash a cup before he could have some coffee. He dug out the tea kettle, washed it, filled it with water, and placed it on the stove. Then he found a match and lit the stove. He turned around and opened the refrigerator, from which he removed a can of Shanghai coffee. The refrigerator, a Westinghouse, was in operation only for two months during the summer; the rest of the year it was not plugged in, and merely served as a cupboard. For one thing, electricity was too costly (it wouldn't have bothered him to hand over an extra ten yuan a month, but he was concerned that people might talk); for another, he normally ate in the cafeteria.

The great hulking object left very little space in the tiny kitchen even to turn around. Geng Er reflected that it might have been better in the long run if the Red Guards had taken the thing along with them while they were on their property confiscation binge.

The pity of it was that they'd gone about their confiscation in such a refined fashion. Perhaps that particular group of Red Guards had been so courteous to him because it was made up of children of his colleagues at the Academy. All they'd done was to open the refrigerator door out of curiosity, turn a few somersaults on his box-spring bed, and dig out some of the Western suits from his trunk. After poking a few jokes at his clothes, they had left. The destruction of his twenty-year collection of newspaper clippings regarding space exploration had pained him at the time, but then saving those really didn't serve any purpose, so why not just commit them to the flames? After all, the Chinese certainly were in no hurry to travel to the moon.

Yet despite the kid-glove treatment, two years after the incident the State Council sent him a letter of apology, which had been formalized with a large red official seal. If anything, that proved an embarrassment to him, for compared to the treatment meted out to many other families, his losses could hardly be considered significant. Some time later a colleague informed him that Premier Zhou had heard reports about the confiscation of property belonging to returned scholars from Europe and America who were working at the Academy, and had ordered that returned technicians and scientists be given favored treatment.

Long Live Premier Zhou! Geng Er silently wished him all the best.

The water was boiling. Geng Er dug around for a moment and located a spoon. He put two scoops of coffee in the pot, replaced the lid, and turned the fire low.

For Premier Zhou he held the greatest respect and admiration. In 1973, just as the Anti–Lin Biao, Anti-Confucius campaign was getting under way, many people were saying privately that although the president of the Academy of Sciences, Guo Moruo, was under attack, the point of the spear was actually aimed at the Premier. Geng Er was concerned for Zhou Enlai, particularly during the first half of 1974, when for several months the Premier made no public appearances. Underground reports were rampant, all of which depressed and disconcerted Geng Er. He was finally able to relax a bit when he read in the newspaper that the Premier was laid up in the hospital.

Geng Er closed his eyes and breathed deeply, letting the aroma of coffee refresh him. He rinsed the tea cup he'd used in the morning, and reminded himself that he'd have to wash all those dishes before Wang Dasao returned. He found the filter he'd bought at the herbal medicine shop and poured his coffee through it.

He carefully carried the cup into the next room, sat down at his desk, and slowly sipped his coffee. His combination living room and study contained only a desk, two chairs, a waste-basket, and a full bookcase. On his desk stood three Christmas cards from America, which he now read once more. He had received them a long time ago, and the senders had all wanted to know what his "present situation" was, but he had never answered any of them. The truth was that he didn't know what to say; present or past situation, it made no difference since there was really nothing worth telling. It dawned on him that these cards had already fulfilled their mission, so what was the use of keeping them around? He gathered them up and threw them in the wastebasket.

Without doubt, America wasted more paper than any other country on earth. Why, in greeting cards alone, there was a congratulatory variety for every imaginable occasion, and con-dolence cards for the passing of a loved one; and people often received get-well cards for minor ailments. Dispensing with all this ceremony in China resulted in savings in time and energy; although . . . although what? Geng Er shook his head without quite knowing why, then took a long drink of coffee.

He saw by the clock on his desk that it was three-thirty. He checked his wristwatch—three-thirty on the nose. At six o'clock he had to be at the home of his colleague Xiao Zhang. During the past couple of years he had rarely visited Xiao Zhang, so the invitation, extended the week before, for New Year's dinner had come as a surprise. Maybe they sympathize with me because I'm alone, and they're afraid that my New

Year's will be dreary, he thought. His first reaction was to refuse and thereby save himself from being reminded of a more recent sorrow. But Xiao Zhang dropped by again only the day before to urge him to come over. The prospect of eating New Year's dinner in the cafeteria was unpleasant (the head cook was on vacation and the apprentice was taking his place in the kitchen; add to that the depressing atmosphere of the nearly deserted cafeteria), so he cheerfully accepted the invitation.

Xiao Zhang was thirty-five or thirty-six years old, but everyone called him "Xiao" because there was another fellow named Zhang at the Academy, whom they called Lao Zhang or "Old" Zhang; in order to avoid confusion, he was stuck with the appellation "Little." He did research in the physics institute, having been a bright graduate of the Shanghai Communications College. Although his origins were far from ideal, he was content with what he was and with his lot, so that during the Cultural Revolution he didn't suffer too much. Geng Er had met him at an academic conference, following which Xiao Zhang came to ask him about some geophysical data, and from then on they got to know each other well. Possibly it was because they worked in different institutes, and because Xiao Zhang didn't live in the Academy dormitory—he and his wife lived in the dormitory of her unit—that he was so eager to associate with Geng Er. In the past he'd often invited Geng Er over to relax and enjoy himself, though in the course of a year it was unusual if he came to Geng Er's dormitory at all.

No matter what, I really should call on them, Geng Er thought as he sipped his coffee. Certainly they've been genuinely concerned about me, and even though Xiao Jin and I didn't get married, Xiao Zhang and his wife have done everything they could.

In the spring of 1971, Mrs. Zhang's cousin Xiao Jin had come to Beijing on a holiday. Since she was staying with the Zhangs, Xiao Zhang made a point of introducing her to Geng Er, but first he told Geng Er all about her. Xiao Jin was thirty, fair-skinned, with rather small eyes. She had recently been widowed, but had no children. "She's a graduate of a normal school, which is roughly the same as being a university student, even though she doesn't really meet the standards you've set." Xiao Zhang couldn't keep from smiling as he said this.

Ai! Not only had Geng Er blushed then, but he grew uneasy thinking about the conversation even now. It harked back to a tremendous blunder he had committed almost the moment he'd set foot in the country, and for which he knew he'd be a laughingstock for the rest of his life. Shortly after he'd taken up his post, one of the unit leaders sought him out for a chat and asked if there was anything he particularly desired. Without thinking, Geng Er blurted out that he hoped to get married at an early date, to which the leader nodded repeatedly without saying a word. Before long a colleague who was passing the time of day with him asked what qualities he envisioned for his ideal wife. Without a moment's hesitation he answered that she should be a college graduate with large eyes and fair skin, and shouldn't be over thirty. How could he have known that this would become common knowledge, and that everyone would snicker and shake their heads, saying that his conditions were far too rigid? When he realized that everyone was talking about him, Geng Er's embarrassment knew no bounds.

And yet his first meeting with Xiao Jin proved very satisfying. She was born and raised in Guilin, and that "land of unsurpassed scenic beauty" seemed to have endowed her with a certain appeal. She was small in stature, had fair skin and an oval face, and her hair was cut in what was commonly called the overseas Chinese fashion. Although her eyes were on the small side, she was well groomed, and Geng Er simply could not tell that she was thirty and had already been married.

Xiao Jin, too, seemed pleased by what she saw, and when Mrs. Zhang proposed that Geng Er take her to the Summer Palace on Worker's Day, she readily agreed and even suggested a place to meet. As expected, their outing turned out very well, and from then on, Geng Er had a standing date to take her out every Sunday.

He tried hard to forget Xiao Qing, but he soon realized that his efforts were in vain, and he could only hope that the shadow of his past would in no way affect his marriage.

The two women were so different that he sometimes found himself subjecting them to comparison. When Xiao Qing had fallen in love she was still young, and the future had held many dreams for her. Xiao Jin, on the other hand, was a mature woman who harbored no illusions. She was primarily concerned with what she could get out of life. She was realistic and practical, and obviously an ideal housewife. She asked the same question about everything: "Is it worth it?" There were times when Geng Er dared not imagine the measure of his own worth in her eyes. From their very first meeting he was aware of how warm and considerate she was toward him. She loved to talk, but on those occasions when Geng Er was in a pensive mood, she managed to keep her tongue in check and sit quietly.

Xiao Jin was a great admirer of Western things, and liked to be taken to Western-style restaurants. And even though to Geng Er the steak might be so well done it was like chewing wax, she would eat it with gusto. And what about the mutton hot pot, of which he never grew tired? Once seemed to be enough for her. Geng Er invited her to his dormitory during the mid-autumn festival for a cup of coffee (it was also his intention to let everyone see that he had found someone). She went over the two rooms carefully, looking at everything and praising his mahogany box-spring bed, his wardrobe, and his refrigerator. She touched them all lovingly and lingered over them all.

"What a beautiful bed! Such fine wood! You really should have brought more furniture with you when you came back."

But Geng Er was embarrassed; he blushed and was at a loss for words. Xiao Jin couldn't have known how much he regretted having shipped this furniture over when he returned to China. For many years it was an emotional burden to him. Xiao Qing had also been aware that he owned a refrigerator, but she had never even wanted to see it. What different women they were!

Geng Er had trouble reconciling the fact that he was Xiao Jin's senior by sixteen years, and for that reason he hesitated to make his feelings known. But Xiao Jin seemed to read his mind and gave him plenty of encouragement. She often hinted, and sometimes commented openly, that he was still robust, that he didn't show his age, and that he walked briskly, like a young man.

Geng Er was also aided by the census check. In 1971, as National Day drew near, out-of-town residents were not being allowed to remain in Beijing. Neighborhood committees had been mobilized to urge visitors who had no official business to leave as soon as possible. Since Xiao Jin had been in Beijing for more than four months, the local neighborhood committee had already been to see her three times and ordered her to return to Guilin before National Day. The day after Xiao Zhang passed this information on, Geng Er asked Xiao Jin to join him for dinner, and he proposed to her in the restaurant. She accepted happily and readily, without the slightest trace of feminine shyness. On the contrary, she urged Geng Er to turn in the marriage request soon, and then she wrote down the date of her birth, her family background, her occupation, and her work history. "I'll be in Guilin waiting for news from you," she said warmly, her small eyes looking at him ardently, her soft white hand holding his. Geng Er squeezed her small hand, and in the midst of the noisy crowd of people, they sat in silence, smiling at each other.

Geng Er arranged for Xiao Jin's train ticket and bought her many gifts. Two days before October First, he went with Xiao Zhang to see her off on the southbound train. Immediately after National Day Geng Er submitted his marriage request. When his colleagues at the institute found out that he was going to marry a pretty little widow, they all congratulated him heartily, and some of the women even offered to help with the wedding. Geng Er was so happy he was even singing a few snatches from a revolutionary opera.

After submitting his request he lived in a state of happy anticipation. Two weeks went by, and his department head informed him that his superiors were giving the request careful consideration, and he would be informed the moment the decision was made. Geng Er was puzzled. Giving it careful consideration? After all, this is me, Geng Er, who's getting married, he thought. Why does someone else need to give the matter consideration? Experience told him that accepting everything as arranged was the best stratagem, so he said nothing. But as 1971 came to a close and no news was forthcoming, he grew anxious. Once he even brazenly asked for some news, and his department head told him that the institute authorities were just then checking into Comrade Jin's family background and that he should be patient. Anger filled his heart, but he remained silent. Xiao Jin continued to write fervent letters, but he had no good news to report to her.

Before long Geng Er was sent to a farm in Jiangxi for six months' labor reform, and the matter was shelved for the time being. Following that, he was given an out-of-town assignment that lasted several months, and by the time he returned it was already the fall of 1972. He had long since lost the courage to ask for news. One political campaign followed another, all of them major events involving the national leadership and the integrity of the nation, so of what importance was one individual's marriage?

One day during a break in the political discussion period, the head of Geng Er's department asked him if he still had any contact with Xiao Jin. The question put him on guard, and he had a feeling of impending disappointment. "I haven't heard from her for a long time. I'm not even sure where she is now," he answered.

His reply seemed to please the department head, who seemed to know what was on Geng Er's mind. "It's for the best if you sever your relationship with her. You see, her background is no good. Her father was a landlord and her husband's status was no better, for his father was one of the Guangxi Clique warlords. Toward the end of the Cultural Revolution her husband was investigated in conjunction with the Cleansing of the Class Ranks, but before the results of the investigation were known, he 'terminated his ties with the Party and the people'—

committed suicide—and so his political status remains unclear. As for her, she was originally a middle-school teacher. In 1970 she was directed to go into the countryside and work on a farm, but she made excuses that her parents' health was poor, so she remained in Guilin. Later on she went off somewhere for a long period of time. For those of us who work in a highly sensitive spot such as the Academy of Sciences, a wife with this sort of background is certainly not ideal. Our superiors are very concerned about your marital situation, and it's on the minds of your colleagues as well . . ."

The department head had quite a bit more to say, but Geng Er heard none of it. He could only congratulate himself that he was old enough to keep his emotions under control. Rather than explode in rage, he actually nodded his head very politely in agreement. But deep down in his heart he cried in despair, Why, why did I have to work in the Academy of Sciences?

At first he felt sorry only for himself, but late at night when everything was quiet and he sat down to write a letter to Xiao Jin, he saw how unjustly she was being treated. Of what crime was she guilty? She was being forced to suffer for the sins of her parents and of her deceased husband. Reportedly she had not responded to Chairman Mao's call, and she stood accused of vanity and cherishing city life. But Geng Er, who had spent time in the countryside as duty demanded, did not have the heart to criticize her for these failings. It was clear, of course, that there was no hope for their union. Geng Er hadn't written to her for a long time, but he was afraid that Xiao Jin would continue to wait in vain and waste her youth. He was also unwilling to divulge the true situation. In the end he told her somewhat ambiguously that his superiors felt that their ages were too disparate and that even he felt strongly that it was an unwise match. He asked for her forgiveness and wished her every happiness.

After mailing the letter he felt that he had let Xiao Jin down, but he also felt that he had been seriously wronged, and he yearned to find a place where he could give vent to his rage. Unhappily, no such place existed. He wasn't willing to reveal his disappointment to his superiors and his colleagues for fear that they would laugh at him for being discouraged just because he couldn't find a wife. Concealing his emotions proved to be the most difficult thing of all.

He soon discovered that he tired very easily and that although he longed for rest, he suffered from insomnia. When he was at work his mind often wandered, and even his memory, of which he had always been so proud, began to fail him. He knew without consulting a physician that he was suffering from a typical case of neurotic depression, for which there was no medication.

Shortly afterward, Lin Biao's attempted coup and death were reported. The official proclamations and the rumors about this perplexing incident drove Geng Er to distraction. He was unclear as to just who was being victimized—he himself, Lin Biao, or possibly Chairman Mao. He felt that he had been deprived of his last remaining shred of faith, and he was as helpless as a blind man who has lost his cane. Then he caught a cold, and had to stay in bed. As he had not been ill for many years, his superiors and colleagues were greatly concerned and showered him with sympathy. He was glad to take a few days of sick leave, even though he knew that there was really nothing wrong with him. He simply needed to rest, to sleep, to lie in bed and do nothing but stare at the ceiling.

He had already recovered and was back on the job when he

received Xiao Jin's reply. Warm and considerate as ever, she alluded to the past with fondness and tried to gloss over her disappointment. She treasured their friendship, she said at the end of her letter, and hoped that they would continue to correspond. When it was clear that she did not reproach him in the least, Geng Er felt somewhat better. Someone as alert as Xiao Jin would have seen the truth—perhaps Xiao Zhang had told her, for he sensed things earlier and more acutely than most people, and he had already found out the actual circumstances of the matter, though he never mentioned it to Geng Er. Geng Er did not believe that Xiao Zhang would blame him, and their meetings were always friendly; still, they no longer got together very often.

Geng Er did a quick calculation and realized that he hadn't been in the Zhang home for precisely two years. "Lingling and Tingting are always asking about you," Xiao Zhang had said to him the previous day. Geng Er and the two little girls had been great friends.

It suddenly occurred to Geng Er that he had to have New Year's presents for the children and that it was now four o'clock. He had long since finished his coffee, so he put the cup back in the kitchen sink. He gave the clothes he was wearing the once-over. His pants were soiled but instead of changing them he decided to put on a pair of Dacron over-trousers. He made sure that his wallet was in the pocket of his padded cotton jacket; put on a cap, a scarf, and gloves; and left. Xiao Zhang lived outside West Gate, but first Geng Er had to ride into the city to buy what he needed.

Except for the big red couplets recently pasted on either side of the entrance to the department store, all the New Year's greetings had revolutionary themes. There was a festive air among the people on the streets, even though there were no special holiday decorations in sight, and the department store was still crowded with customers. Geng Er was surprised to see so many people in the same predicament as he, still buying presents on the last night of the year.

He went first to the confection counter, where he eyed the tins of cookies in the showcase as he stood in line.

"What do you want?" asked a clerk whose eyelids were so droopy he seemed about to fall asleep.

"I'd like a tin of Taikang Cookies," he said, pointing to the largest and most attractive tin.

"They're not for sale!" the clerk said impatiently, raising his eyebrows and sneering at him.

"Well . . ." Geng Er wasn't sure what he should do now. "Well, what kinds are for sale?"

"Do you want expensive ones?" The clerk's eyes were now wide open as he sized up his customer.

"Yes. Yes, I do."

The clerk took out a tin of Tianshan Cookies. "This is eight-fifty."

"Are they rationed?" asked a customer with an out-of-town accent who was standing behind Geng Er. He closed in and enviously touched the tin.

"Of course not. Ration coupons aren't required for expensive items," another customer interjected, with a sarcastic ring. "Eight-fifty! There couldn't be more than two catties in the tin. Cookies in bulk sell for less than two yuan a catty!"

Just as Geng Er was about to say something, a hand reached in alongside him.

"Let me have a tin too!"

Everyone turned to look. It was a soldier, holding a ten-yuan bill in his other hand.

"All right, all right!" the clerk answered, momentarily revitalized.

"I want a box of chocolates, too," Geng Er quickly added. "That is, if you have them in metal tins."

"None in metal tins. How about those wrapped in tin foil? They're from Shanghai and make excellent gifts."

"All right, they're fine. Give me twenty."

"Twenty!" The clerk's eyes were really wide open now. "These are all we have left." He placed the entire supply on the counter.

"All right, that'll do," said Geng Er, taking his money out of his pocket. "Could I trouble you to wrap it all up together?"

Geng Er quickly picked up his parcel and virtually flew from the confection counter and the stares of everyone present. Fortunately there weren't many people at the salted meats counter. He purchased several catties of Hunan salted meat and Cantonese-style sausage. Then he bought some apples at a fruit stand. By now his hands were full and it was getting late, so he left the store. He attached one package to the handlebars and carefully tied the rest to the book rack on the back of his bicycle. Then he slowly rode west.

The sky turned dark and cold before six o'clock. The city itself was bustling, but after Geng Er left the West Gate district the streets were much quieter. The vehicles on the road seemed to be moving a little faster. The bicyclists rode with their noses and mouths covered by white masks, as they leaned over their handlebars and pedaled energetically in anticipation of their year-end family dinners. Geng Er let quite a few of them pass him, feeling that he was probably the only one who wasn't in any particular hurry.

The large dormitory complex where the Zhangs lived looked somewhat unfamiliar, since he hadn't been there for two years, but he quickly found their place and parked his bicycle by the door.

Xiao Zhang stuck his head out. "Lao Geng, you made it!" He hurried out the door.

"Say there, Xiao Zhang! Am I late?"

"No, we're just getting ready to eat!" Xiao Zhang came out to help Geng Er with his bundles. "It was enough just for you to come. You didn't have to bring all these packages too!"

"It's New Year's—it's for the children. How are they?"

No sooner had he asked the question than they appeared in the doorway, both dressed in fancy new sweaters. The older one remained standing by the door, but the younger one ran over to Geng Er and tugged on his coat. She looked up at him, and said, "Uncle Geng, you haven't been to see us for a long time."

"Ah, Lingling, look how tall you've grown!" Geng Er bent over and cheerfully stroked her little braid. "Are you in school now?"

"Not yet," her father answered for her. "She was born on September first, and since there were too few openings this year, she didn't qualify. She'll have to wait till next fall. By then she'll be seven years old, so there shouldn't be any problem."

"That's a shame, but then starting school a year late doesn't make that much difference."

"That's right," Xiao Zhang agreed. "Later, when she goes out to the farm, if she's a little older it will be to her advantage, since she'll be able to wield the hoe better."

"Uncle Geng," the older daughter called out to their guest. She was demure and a little self-conscious.

"Ah, Tingting, I hardly recognized you. You're getting prettier all the time. What grade are you in now?"

"Fourth," she answered shyly, as she stood aside to let everyone else pass.

As he stepped inside Geng Er could smell the sweet-and-sour pork and could hear food sizzling in the pan.

Xiao Zhang's one-and-a-half room apartment—one room was so small that Zhang jokingly referred to it as half a room—was filled to capacity with furniture, quite the opposite of Geng Er's. The larger room measured only ten by ten but the Zhangs had squeezed in a bed, a desk that also served as a dinner table, a bookcase, and a sewing machine. The space beneath the bed was crammed full, and things were even hanging from the ceiling. The smaller room held only a bed.

"Please have a seat," said Xiao Zhang, as he placed the parcels on the bed. Geng Er put the package of salted meats in the only unoccupied space, on top of the sewing machine. Xiao Zhang sat down alongside the table, which had been placed at the head of the bed, thereby eliminating the need for a chair. The two girls immediately nestled up to him, one on either side. The dinner table had been set and two dishes had already been placed in the center: a steaming bowl of stewed meat and one of meat and vegetables.

"How has your wife been lately?"

"Fine, just fine; about the same as the rest of us, spending her time poring over documents, trying to understand every word." As he was speaking, Mrs. Zhang walked in carrying a plate of food, a broad grin on her face.

"Mr. Geng, how are you?"

"Fine, thank you, just fine."

He rose to his feet, but before he could finish what he was saying, another woman carrying a plate of food came into the room. It was Xiao Jin. Geng Er was so surprised he was at a loss for words and just stood there dumbly.

"How are you, Lao Geng?" The smile on her face could not entirely hide her nervousness.

"When . . . did you arrive in Beijing?" It took him some time before he was able to pick up the conversation.

"Just two days ago," Mrs. Zhang answered for her cousin.

"Come on, sit down," said Xiao Zhang, ceremoniously.

Mrs. Zhang put the plates on the table and made Xiao Jin sit down.

"Jin Jie,* you don't have to come out into the kitchen; I'll bring the soup when it's ready. Go ahead and see that everyone is served."

Mrs. Zhang wiped her hands on her apron and went back to the kitchen.

At first glance, Xiao Jin seemed unchanged. Her clothing was a bit more colorful and better made, her short hair was very neat, and when she smiled her dimples were as captivating as ever. She was just as unaffected, but her eyes didn't seem as clear and spirited as they had in the past. Then Geng Er noticed wrinkles at the corners of her eyes. We're all getting older! He sighed inwardly.

"You seem slimmer," he said.

"Really?" There was a hint of sadness in her voice. At the same time she unconsciously tidied up her already smooth short hair. Tingting brought out a pot of rice, and Xiao Jin

---

*Literally "Elder Sister Jin."

began to fill everyone's bowl. Xiao Zhang went to the bookcase for a bottle of cherry wine.

"Well, what have we here! Where did you get that?" Geng Er asked enviously. He didn't care much for sweet wines, but things always seem more precious when they're scarce, and wine like that could not be bought on the open market.

"Ha! It wasn't easy!" Xiao Zhang said proudly as he searched for a bottle opener. "The fellow in our institute from England, Lao Luo—do you know who I mean? Well, around the first of the year an old schoolmate of his from England came to Beijing to visit some relatives, and he stopped off to see him while he was in the vicinity. On a sudden inspiration, I asked Luo to see if his guest could buy a few things for me at the Friendship Store, and that's how I managed to get my hands on this bottle of wine and the Shanghai sweaters the girls are wearing. Those sweaters cost the same as the ones on the market, but they're of much better quality!"

A few moments later Mrs. Zhang carried in a potful of soup cooked with a whole chicken. The table wasn't big enough to begin with, and since the two children liked the idea of eating by themselves, Zhang finally had them take their food into the adjoining room. When Mrs. Zhang had removed her apron and was seated at the table opposite Xiao Jin, Zhang raised his glass and toasted Geng Er. "Here we go, bottoms up! Good luck to everyone!"

"Here's hoping that everything goes well for everyone this New Year's holiday!" Xiao Jin added.

Neither of the women was accustomed to drinking wine; Mrs. Zhang managed to drink half a glass, while Xiao Jin took only one sip and set her glass down as though she had something on her mind. Geng Er couldn't tell what she was thinking and was embarrassed to ask what had brought her to Beijing. He had received a letter from her only the month before, and there was no mention of any plans for a visit. Even more important to him was how long she was planning to stay this time, but he had no opportunity to ask. The talk around the table was mainly of national affairs, such as Zhou Enlai's continued role as helmsman, and the formal appearance on the scene of Deng Xiaoping.

"With older men in charge, we can all take it a little easier," Xiao Zhang commented with feeling. "There have just been too many ups and downs these past few years, and every time the leftists are in power we're all in for a rough time."

"You'd better keep that sort of rightist talk in the home, or you'll wind up wearing a label!" Mrs. Zhang warned her husband. She was a very affable woman, short and stout, her face never without a smile.

"Hai! Don't you worry. At the institute I've always tested the winds and I'm right there with every change of course," Xiao Zhang said. "When they were integrating the archaeological excavation of the Zhou dynasty tombs with the Anti–Lin Biao, Anti-Confucius campaign, the statement I wrote was in demand even by the Propaganda Section."

"Xiao Zhang really does have a knack for writing," praised Geng Er. Whenever he had to write political criticism he could never think of what to say. He couldn't help admiring Zhang's talent.

"You're being too polite," Xiao Zhang protested humbly. "I'm not in the same league with the young fellows in the archaeological institute. In all honesty, they've dug up quite a few objects these past few years, and that's proved very stimulating to them. The pity is, they lag behind in arranging, laboratory analysis, and preservation techniques, so some of the objects have changed color after being unearthed, and may have even fallen apart."

Mrs. Zhang suddenly laughed. "My, I don't know how you integrated the Anti–Lin Biao, Anti-Confucius campaigns, but it was quite something at our unit. The last time we had a big criticism meeting, one of the workers got up to speak. He began by reading a prepared text, but the more aroused he grew, the more impromptu his talk became. He said that Lin the Bald One had predicted that New China was going to revert back to Confucian times, where the majority of people would be slaves and the minority would act as the nobility. 'Comrades, how can we accept this kind of reactionary talk?' Those of us at the foot of the podium naturally began shouting our unqualified rejection of such a policy. But then we glanced at one another, wondering when and where Lin Biao could have uttered such absurdities as those!"

"It's the same everywhere, people aping others," Geng Er commented with a smile.

"You'll be all right if you just get on the bandwagon quickly," said Xiao Zhang as he refilled Geng Er's glass. "Come on, Lao Geng, this is what really counts: 'Here is wine, let us sing / For man's life is short.' "

And so they ate and chatted, holding nothing back, passing the time pleasantly. Geng Er discovered that Xiao Jin wasn't as lively and talkative as before; she was more demure and dignified, and lovelier than ever. He hoped that her stay in Beijing, like her last visit, could be an extended one, and he longed to spend that time with her. Not having seen her for more than a year, and now finding himself sitting beside her, he felt not only excitement but comfort as well; it was as though the accumulated fatigue had been erased in a moment. As he gazed at her pink cheeks and her small hand holding the chopsticks, his heart began pounding faster and faster. A great many visions crowded into his mind, particularly of two days he and Xiao Jin had spent together in Guilin.

As though on cue, Mrs. Zhang began to talk about Guilin, where she had spent her youth. She still had cherished memories of that beautiful region.

"Do you still go to Great Dipper Crag or to the place they just discovered, Reed Flute Crag?" she asked her cousin. But before Xiao Jin had a chance to answer, Mrs. Zhang put down her chopsticks and continued enviously, "I wonder when I'll be able to go to Guilin again. How lucky you are not to have to worry about being sent down to the countryside anymore. As a matter of fact, as I see it, you don't ever have to worry about work assignments at all."

Xiao Jin quickly cut her short, "Why not find an excuse this summer to take a few days off?" Then she turned to Geng Er and said with a smile, "Guilin is lovelier than ever. If you're sent to Guangxi on assignment again, make sure you come to Guilin for another visit."

"How could it not be lovely!" Xiao Zhang interjected. "It's one of the places that's on every foreign tourist's itinerary."

At the word "tourist," Xiao Jin asked Geng Er, "Do you remember Han Suyin? I read that she recently gave a speech at Hong Kong University and had many good things to say about China."

"Of course I remember." Geng Er smiled. He too had seen the news item, and he even recalled the subject of her speech:

"How I Came to Know China." Indeed, how could he have forgotten Han Suyin, even though he had never talked to anyone else about seeing her.

Early in the summer of 1973 he'd gone to Guangxi province on a geological inspection, and when his work was done, the young colleague who had accompanied him suggested that they stay over for a couple of days so that the young man could visit his parents. Geng Er was glad to accommodate him, and arranged to wait for him in nearby Guilin. Geng Er immediately went to see Xiao Jin, who was overjoyed to see him. He met her parents, and then he and Xiao Jin discussed how to spend their windfall of two days together. They decided to take the spectacular river trip from Guilin to Yangsuo, so early the next day they lined up at the pier to buy tickets and were fortunate enough to be able to crowd onto one of the boats. Once through the mountain pass and onto the Li River, they were entranced by the magnificent scenery on both shores. Geng Er had traveled to nearly every spot in North America and had seen many natural wonders, but never had he been so moved.

The clear water of the Li River, the white clouds, the blue sky, and the mountain peaks reflected in the water were like another world. Suddenly Xiao Jin nudged him, bringing him back to reality. Another boat, less than a hundred meters away, was rapidly coming upon them. A man and a woman were seated in the prow: the man dark-skinned and with a high nose, looking somewhat Indian; the woman obviously part Asian. There was a ring of people, all dressed like mid-level cadre members, standing around this foreign couple, and a fancy tea service, including watermelon and other snacks, was laid out on the table before them.

The woman's face looked familiar to Geng Er. "Ah, that's right," he said softly to Xiao Jin, suddenly recognizing her. "That's Han Suyin. I've seen her in the movies and on television."

"Oh, really?" Xiao Jin's eyes grew wide and her eyebrows arched as she stared at the foreign tourists. "There was a newspaper article about Comrade Jiang Qing meeting her. If that's the case, then that fellow who looks like an Indian must be her husband. I thought that since his name was Lu, he must be Chinese."

Han Suyin and her husband were pointing at the scenic wonders around them, and delight was written on their faces. Their boat soon passed the tour boat, and Geng Er quickly put them out of his mind. He was aware only of the magnificent scenery and Xiao Jin's description of the lovely sights they were passing: Ginkgo Nut Sandbar, Lady in the Mirror . . .

A stirring among the other passengers roused him. The special boat was lying dead in the water directly ahead of them. The glamorous Han Suyin could be seen talking and laughing animatedly.

"What's going on, comrade?" he asked the person next to him.

"It looks like the motor on the foreign tourists' boat has broken down, and our captain is going over to help them fix it."

"We're going to be late getting to Yangsuo," another passenger said anxiously, as he looked at his wristwatch.

The motor on the special boat was soon running again, and it continued on its way. As the distance between the two boats lengthened rapidly, it was obvious that the regular tour boat was not moving at all! The passengers were then informed that their trip was cancelled because the motor had been removed and placed in the foreign visitors' boat. Geng Er still recalled the disappointment and anger on the faces of the tourists.

"That sort of thing happens all the time," Mrs. Zhang commented indifferently, after hearing Geng Er's story.

"The problem was that most of the people on our boat were travelers in a hurry to get somewhere."

Xiao Zhang shook his head at Geng Er's stubbornness. "Have you forgotten, Lao Geng?" he asked with a smile. "Even though every word Lin Biao ever spoke is now poison, there is a great deal of truth in what he said at Tiananmen: 'The losses suffered in the Cultural Revolution were very, very small, while the rewards were very, very great.' Why? Because political rewards are the most important of all. What does it matter that twenty or thirty people couldn't get to Yangsuo? But it matters a great deal to have Han Suyin say something good about China abroad."

"But, the problem is . . ."

And yet Geng Er couldn't say just what the problem was. He wondered how Han Suyin felt about the incident.

At nine-thirty, after the guests had finished their fruit, Geng Er rose and reluctantly said he had to leave. He had hoped to broach the subject of seeing Xiao Jin again, but the opportunity to speak to her had never arisen.

"Lao Geng, come over and see us whenever you've nothing to do," Zhang said sincerely. "My wife and I are very informal. The children, too, look forward to seeing you; they want to study English with you someday."

"I'll come for sure," he said quickly as he patted little Lingling's shoulder. He was a little ashamed that he'd consciously avoided the family for two whole years.

Xiao Jin went into the adjoining room to fetch an intricately woven bamboo basket, which she gave to Geng Er. Inside the basket were a jar of Guilin spiced fermented bean curd and a bottle of liquor. "I didn't bring you anything special, just a couple of local products," she said softly.

"Xiao Jin . . ." He looked at the basket, then at her, so moved for the moment that he didn't know how to express his gratitude. The little bit of wine she'd drunk had brought a pinkness to her cheeks and a sparkle to her eyes. The tiny wrinkles around her eyes heightened the expressiveness of her features, so that her smile held even greater charm. As for Geng Er, the wine and an evening of happiness had brought a warmth to his body and a lightness to his feet. At that moment he made up his mind to send in another marriage request. This time he'd write a letter to Premier Zhou and, if necessary, get his old classmate from America to help. Upon his return from the assignment in Guangxi he had planned to pursue the matter seriously, but unfortunately the Anti–Lin Biao, Anti-Confucius campaign had been mounted, and he'd had no choice but to let the matter lie. He now rebuked himself for having moved so slowly.

"I'll see you out to the main gate," Xiao Jin said as she picked up her cap and gloves.

Xiao Zhang had already put on his cap and coat, but he quickly took off his cap. "Well, then, I won't be seeing you out. Lao Geng, be sure to come over when you have the time."

Although it was below freezing, with Xiao Jin beside him Geng Er didn't feel the cold. His heart seemed to be beating in rhythm with the little bamboo basket swaying from the handlebars of his bicycle. The distant sound of firecrackers accentuated the stillness of this New Year's eve.

Geng Er had grown accustomed to silence and loneliness,

but only at that moment, as he walked beside Xiao Jin, gently resting his hand on her shoulder, was he finally able to savor the peace and security that are born of silence. In this rare mood of happiness, he had even less desire to speak, and Xiao Jin, too, conscious of her own feelings, remained quiet so as not to shatter this peaceful moment.

When they reached the street beyond the West Gate, Xiao Jin finally broke the silence. "Lao Geng," she said in a weak and hesitant voice, as she slowed her pace.

"Hm?"

He looked down affectionately at her and gently pulled her closer to him.

"I . . ." She started to speak, but stopped with a frightened look in her eyes, as though she were searching for something, or making an appeal, or even performing an act of penance.

"What's wrong, Xiao Jin?" Geng Er came to a halt, bent over slightly, and looked at her anxiously.

She turned away abruptly. Then with great difficulty she managed to speak the words "I'm married."

"Married?" he echoed. The hand he had placed on her shoulder fell limply to his side.

She quickly turned and looked up at him.

"You're angry," she said, frowning. "You think I wasn't willing to wait. But I had no choice!" Her voice was mournful, but it also carried a note of protest.

"It's all my fault," Geng Er said at last, feeling utterly spent.

"Don't talk like that." Seeing how dejected he was, Xiao Jin felt even worse, but she tried to smooth things over by saying gently, "My background is no good, and to have gone on waiting would have been harmful to you."

Geng Er sensed that his tone had been too harsh, and felt

that he had let her down badly. How could she have waited any longer? He reproached himself bitterly. I never gave her enough hope—I was too selfish.

He was suddenly aware of the bone-chilling cold. He started to move again, supporting Xiao Jin with one hand and pushing his bicycle along with the other.

"I'm glad you got married, Xiao Jin." He forced himself to be calm and was proud of his self-control. "What you've done is absolutely right, and I wish you happiness."

Xiao Jin walked with her head down, not making a sound.

"Your husband . . . where is he now?" Geng Er tried to sound casual, but the word "husband" stuck in his throat. "Look, I may have lost a prospective wife, but I've gained a friend."

Xiao Jin looked at him gratefully. "He's an old cadreman. He's been an invalid for more than ten years. His two children work in the Northeast and they both have their own families, so he doesn't care at all if people criticize him about his second marriage. The authorities knew he needed someone to take care of him in his old age, and naturally they won't be sending me out into the countryside."

Poor woman! Geng Er loved her more at this moment than ever before.

"Why didn't he come with you to Beijing?" he asked. "Sometimes a change of scenery is good for a sick person."

"He'll be here tomorrow," she said weakly.

Tomorrow! Geng Er was so completely taken by surprise that his heel nearly got caught in the rear wheel of his bicycle. Why hadn't they come together? He nearly blurted out the question, but he saw the look of hopelessness and surrender on Xiao Jin's face.

They walked on in silence.

"Xiao Jin, you're a brave woman. I'm sure your husband will be good to you. When he gets here, give me a phone call and I'll give him a nice welcome."

"Oh, Lao Geng . . ." She halted abruptly and shook her head. "I don't think we should see each other again."

Not see each other again! The words struck at his heart.

"Lao Geng, I want you to understand." She was almost imploring him. "I couldn't take it; I just know I couldn't take it!"

Xiao Jin suddenly lost her composure, and tears welled up in her eyes. She didn't bother to wipe them away, but just let them run down her cheeks.

"I won't go any farther with you," she said at last.

Geng Er grasped her shoulder tightly. "I'll see you back," he said. But Xiao Jin shook her head resolutely, wiped the tears from her face, and pulled away from his grasp. She looked up at him once more and said softly, "Goodbye." Her footsteps got faster and faster, and finally she lowered her head and ran into one of the alleys.

For a long time Geng Er stood looking down the deserted street where she had just walked. From somewhere came the sputter of exploding firecrackers and the gleeful shouts of children. But for Geng Er, there was only loneliness ahead.

Nixon's
Press Corps

The bugle calls blaring from the loudspeakers that greeted our arrival at school in the morning seemed to be louder and more insistent than usual. Just as we were wondering what it was all about, one of the teachers told us that an emergency meeting of all departments had been called. My husband and I hurried over to the large classroom in which such meetings were usually held. It was already packed with teachers and workers. Lao He, the head of the Department Revolutionary Committee, and Lao Diao, the delegate from the Workers' Propaganda Corps, were sitting alone in the front row; Lao He was leaning over and listening intently as Lao Diao, head bent and eyes crinkled, whispered into his ear. As always, my husband and I silently went our separate ways to join colleagues from our own teaching groups.

"Why are we having another general meeting?" I asked a colleague as I sat down.

"I hear it's on account of Nixon's press corps. It seems they're actually coming here," she whispered back.

This news eased my concern. I leaned back in my chair and waited for the meeting to begin. As long as they weren't launching some political campaign or purging someone, I had nothing to worry about. In preparation for Nixon's forthcoming visit, a general study of all pertinent documents had begun three months earlier. The visit had already become a familiar and accepted thing. One would think that after twenty years of attacking "American Imperialism" as the number one enemy, it would be difficult for people to change their way of thinking to such an extent that they would shake hands and fraternize with the President of the United States. But after an intensive reading of all the circulated documents, their thoughts began to fall in line with what they read. No one ever publicly questioned the contradictory statements or this about-face in Communist policy. When it was announced that Nixon's press corps would be passing through Nanjing, the provincial and metropolitan commissioners made elaborate preparations for the visit. Even the street committees were given sample questions that the correspondents might ask, so that everyone could practice giving appropriate answers.

The loudspeakers stopped promptly at eight, and we all checked our watches.

Lao He was the first to address us. "Good morning, comrades! By direction of the provincial authorities, we have called this meeting to complete preparations for receiving Nixon's press corps. The eighty-member press group traveling with Nixon may pass through Nanjing tomorrow for a one-day visit, so we must be ready. Today we will suspend all normal activities in order to have a general clean-up and tidy up the lawns. All laboratory equipment must be cleaned and labeled in both Chinese and English; if necessary, get some help from the Foreign Languages Section. We believe that the reporters will be in Nanjing for the day only, so the possibility of a visit to our school is quite remote. But as Chairman Mao has taught us, 'Do not fight unprepared battles.' Therefore, we will proceed with preparations in order to be ready for any and all contingencies. We will now ask Lao Diao, Chairman Mao's good worker from the Propaganda Corps, to say a few words to us."

Lao Diao stood up slowly. His small eyes coldly swept over the hall. He cleared his throat loudly and placed one foot on the chair beside Lao He. With his right hand on his raised knee and his left hand resting on his hip, he was the very picture of self-assurance and arrogance. Not a sound was heard in the classroom, as all eyes were on his raised leg. He reminded me of the villain, Diao Deyi, in the revolutionary Peking opera *Shajiabang.*

Lao Diao began with the usual line about the world revolutionary movements signaling the end of the road for American imperialism. Then he said that Nixon had been forced to come begging for peace, and he repeated some of the standard doctrines and policies. Then he reminded everyone: "It is of the utmost importance for us to grasp the characteristics of these reporters. They have their 'three excesses'—an excess of running around, an excess of questions, and an excess of picture taking. But we have our ways of dealing with them: We must maintain an attitude neither overbearing nor humble, neither too approachable nor too distant, neither . . . er, er . . . in other words, if we maintain an attitude of 'three neithers' in dealing with their 'three excesses,' we shall remain invincible."

Suddenly he raised his voice and declared emphatically, "Don't go milling about on the streets tomorrow unless you have important business! There are some who must pay special attention to this, who must behave themselves and refrain from untoward conduct!"

At first I didn't understand what he was talking about. But my face burned when it dawned on me that I might be the object of this veiled warning. I didn't dare look up, for fear that I might meet other people's eyes. I felt so uneasy that I was barely able to sit still. This kind of oblique attack—mentioning no names, but letting one "find one's own seat"—was devastatingly effective. Protesting one's innocence was interpreted as proof of a guilty conscience, so the only thing to do was to swallow the whole thing, no matter how distasteful.

After the general meeting we separated into various discussion groups. While the leader of our group was off receiving his instructions, Xiao Wei, our newsmonger, whose wife had just come from Beijing to visit him, took the opportunity to let us in on a bit of gossip. Rumor had it that during Kissinger's second visit, a woman had dashed out to accost him with a written complaint as his car was passing along Chang'an Avenue. She was immediately hustled off by plainclothesmen and jailed as a counterrevolutionary. The woman's husband was an old Party cadreman who must have been purged during the Cultural Revolution. Evidently she tried to enlist Kissinger's help in bringing up his case for reconsideration.

"She had a lot of nerve but very little sense," Xiao Wei said. "She should have known that they wouldn't let anyone get close to a foreign visitor, especially Kissinger!"

Although this was only a rumor and there was no indication that the woman had been an overseas Chinese, or a returnee from the United States like me, I played it cautiously anyway. As soon as the discussion began I stood up and declared that, except for going directly to and from the classroom, I would not budge from my home all the next day, not even to go to the market. A rightist in the group also made a similar declaration. Afterwards, as we were cleaning up, our group leader came up and patted my shoulder. "Don't be so touchy, Xiao Xin, Lao Diao didn't necessarily mean you."

My only response was a forced smile.

When we went home at noon, both my husband and I were feeling depressed. We ate our lunch in silence.

"We won't even be going to the market tomorrow," I said, "so you'd better go now before you return to work. Just pick up anything—a vegetable or two will be enough."

He was somewhat taken aback for a moment, but he nodded, and went out with the market basket. I was too weary and dispirited even to clear the table, so I just sat there in a daze until a knock at the door brought me around.

"Who is it?" I asked as I opened the door. It was Xiao Miao, a member of our neighborhood committee.

"Xin Laoshi, have you finished lunch?"

"Yes, come in." I made way for her. "Is there something on your mind?"

"Yes," she said solemnly, ignoring my invitation. "We've received orders to clean up the courtyard because Nixon's press corps is coming tomorrow. We are to pull up the weeds, remove the litter from all the nooks and crannies, and . . ." Here she hesitated. "We also have to take down all the drying racks over the windows. They're afraid the foreign visitors will find them an eyesore."

"Take down all the drying racks?" Although this struck me as funny to the point of absurdity, I was unable to laugh.

"Xiao Miao," I said, "with all the famous scenic and historic sites in Nanjing, why would the reporters take the time to come to this isolated area during a one-day visit to the city? And if by chance they happened to pass by here, they will be sitting in cars. And even if they were to stand on top of the cars they still could not see through our gate, to this building four rows back. They wouldn't even be able to see the roof, let alone the windows!"

"I'm just acting on orders from the neighborhood committee." She sighed, spreading her hands in a gesture of helplessness. "I have to take mine down even though it was put up only last month."

I couldn't encourage her to refuse to tear hers down, but I shook my head to express my opposition. We had gone through a lot of trouble to put up our rack two years before. My husband went all the way to the old Confucius Temple area to buy the bamboo poles, and since wire was not available in the markets, I begged a colleague to get me a small roll of it from his laboratory. Then my husband and I spent almost an entire day putting up a rack with three crosspieces outside our south window. It was sturdily built and strong enough to sun a pair of quilts. But two years of wind and rain had already rusted the wires, and if we tore the rack down now we would never be able to put it up again.

"I can't take ours down," I declared stubbornly. "You have my word that I won't hang any clothes out tomorrow, but I simply can't take it down. If I did I wouldn't be able to put it up again. Where would I hang our clothes to dry then? After all, Nixon's reporters are people too. It's unlikely they would say anything when they saw the racks. And if they did, we could take the opportunity to 'reeducate' them and teach them a thing or two!"

Xiao Miao had no answer to that. She just looked distressed

and waved her hands. "All right, but don't say I didn't notify you."

That afternoon as I walked through the dormitory gate on my way home from work I saw all the elderly people cleaning up the yard. Some were raking leaves, others were removing dead grass. Because of the cold, they were so bundled up in heavy clothing their movements appeared even slower and clumsier than usual. The drying racks for the first row of houses facing the road had all vanished. As I walked farther in I saw that most of the racks in the next row had already been taken down, and the rest were being dismantled. The people were working in sullen silence. I was relieved to see that our rack was still safe and untouched, although those around it were gone. One neighbor was just removing the last piece of wood from his rack; he broke it off with a resounding crack and threw the pieces to the ground without a glance. Our rack stood out in lonely splendor in the deepening dusk. I didn't know whether to feel proud or apprehensive.

My husband and son came home before long. As soon as he entered the door my husband cried, "This is sheer madness—a single word and everyone is dismantling them! Just now someone asked me, 'Are you really going to leave yours up?' I could barely keep from asking him, 'Why are you tearing yours down? If we all refused, what could they do about it?'"

"That's enough," I interrupted, glancing at the child.

He immediately dropped the subject.

"Be a good boy and go play in the other room. Mommy will call you as soon as dinner is ready."

With the child out of the way, my husband followed me into the kitchen and demanded, "How about it? Do we tear ours down or not?"

"Of course we don't!" I declared indignantly. "Just because of Nixon's visit, they want us to slap our own faces! The whole country has been frantic for nearly three months, and, now, just because some members of his press corps might pass through here for a day, we're supposed to turn the place upside down for them. We're not even free to go out on the streets! What makes them think I'd want to see the reporters anyway? I'm not even interested in Nixon himself! I still remember his disgraceful performance on television in the midst of the 1952 presidential campaign. He dragged in his dog, Checkers, to get sympathy for his defense against bribery charges. My American roommate was so disgusted that she called him 'political garbage!' Since we're never trusted and we can't afford to protest, we can let an inanimate object like our drying rack stand up for us. The most they can do is tear it to pieces."

My husband tried to soothe me. "All right, all right, we won't tear it down. Just don't make yourself ill. Get dinner ready while I clean up the yard."

We had made our decision, yet I was so distracted I couldn't cook properly. The rice was burned and the spinach was raw. Neither of us had any appetite, and we couldn't find anything to talk about, so we hurried through the meal in silence. Only our son, in his innocence, was his usual self, eating heartily and chattering away.

I had just cleared the table and was about to pour some water to bathe the boy's feet, when my husband rushed in from the other room in great agitation.

"Gao Sao is coming this way, probably to our house. I can't bear that woman, so you'd better talk to her. If she's here about the drying rack, don't argue with her; just take it down!"

I grew uneasy at the mention of Gao Sao's name. It had

never occurred to me that this affair would warrant a personal visit from the chairwoman of the neighborhood committee of our dormitory area. She came from a good background—before Liberation her family had been impoverished, I was told—and her husband was a laborer and a Party member. Ever since the founding of the school she and her family had lived in our dormitory gatehouse, and she was given the responsibility of delivering messages. Though she was still under forty, she was experienced and capable, especially in handling purges within the dormitory. When she attacked the women, the old, and the weak she was truly awesome. Because of her good background, she'd felt free to bear six children, one after the other, but since her husband's wages were insufficient to support them all, they relied on welfare from the state to get by. No shining example of planned parenthood herself, she was nonetheless a staunch supporter of birth control and an eloquent advocate of abortion. She had had little education, but had been born with a glib tongue, and with her high-pitched voice and caustic remarks, no woman was her match. Mao Zedong said that women hold up half the sky, and it seemed to me that in the corner of earth where our dormitory was located, Gao Sao held it up single-handedly.

"Stay here and don't come out," I said as I pushed my husband back into the room. I hurriedly wiped my hands, put my son's shoes back on his feet, and scooted him into the other room. Just as I shut the door behind me, there was a knock on the front door.

Sure enough, there stood Gao Sao.

"Xin Laoshi, have you already had dinner?"

Her words were polite, but her face was cold and unsmiling. With her hands held behind her back, she looked me over from head to toe to show that she meant business and was not to be trifled with.

"Yes, I have," I answered. My heart was thumping wildly, and I could hear my own breathing, but I remained standing in the doorway, unwilling to give way.

"Are you here because of the drying rack?" I decided to come right to the point.

"That's right. Yours is the only one left in the entire dormitory, and if it's not taken down you'll be putting us in an awkward position with the authorities."

Naturally, I repeated the reasons I had given Xiao Miao that morning. But Gao Sao proved a formidable opponent. She said nothing about the possibility of the reporters' passing along our road, but stressed instead the importance of discipline within the revolutionary ranks. She even quoted many of Mao Zedong's sayings, so that in the end, my refusal to dismantle the rack became a political issue. Political pressure is too heavy a burden to accept lightly, and so my anger mounted as I listened to the harangue. Curiously enough, the overall effect was to quiet me down.

Finally, I said calmly, "I don't think you should make so much of this. After all, it's only a small matter, and my refusal to tear the thing down isn't unreasonable. In discussing any issue, one must begin with the major premise, which in the present case is that we should put our best foot forward for our foreign guests. There is no problem here, because I am in complete agreement with the premise. The question is this: What is wrong with drying racks? Even in America there are still many people who hang their clothes out to dry in their backyards . . ."

"I don't know what they do in America, and I don't care!"

she interrupted me with a wave of her hand. "This is China, and we do things the Chinese way."

This argument shamed and distressed me. I stared at her and my cheeks burned as I listened to her high-pitched shouts. The neighbor opposite us gingerly opened her door a crack and stuck her head out, but she quickly closed the door when she saw Gao Sao.

"Nobody knows whether the foreign visitors will pass by here or not, but even if they don't, tearing down a drying rack is at most a small sacrifice for the revolution."

"The state does not advocate unnecessary sacrifices!"

Compared to her strident voice, the tone of my protest was low and my voice was small, shaky, and very weak.

"If the foreign visitors come through and you're the only family whose drying rack is still standing, we in the Party cadre will have to bear the onus of your refusal to carry out our orders. And even if they don't come, what will the other people say? 'Xin Laoshi was right in refusing to tear it down!' It will make it difficult for us to carry on in this area in the future."

I felt like shouting that she was being selfish and thinking only of herself. But she was no one to tangle with. I restrained myself with such force that I trembled all over. There was a sudden pain in my chest, and I couldn't breathe. I pressed my hand against my chest, and, remembering my husband's admonition, decided to give up the argument. I could never get the upper hand with her.

"I'm not going to tear it down," I told her. "If you want it torn down, do it yourself. And you can be responsible for putting it back up when the foreign visitors have gone!"

She was stunned.

"How can I take it down for you?" She quickly changed her tune. "To welcome foreign visitors and clean up the environment is a voluntary action by the revolutionary masses; the Party would never force it on anyone. If you don't tear it down, then the onus is on you, and if anything happens, don't say that we didn't try to carry out our responsibility!"

I hadn't the strength to answer. I just stared at her inverted triangle of a face, which seemed to be growing longer and sharper; her eyes were as arrogant and cold as Lao Diao's.

"Then that's that!" She spat out the words and walked away with her arms behind her back, her head held high. The hard nylon soles of her cloth shoes tapped a sharp tattoo on the cement outside. I shut the door.

That night I didn't sleep well. I woke with a start several times.

The next day passed quietly and uneventfully. On the third day we heard that Nixon's press corps had shown no interest in Nanjing and had gone directly to Hangzhou. Two French reporters were the only ones who stopped over, and they had merely strolled around New Market Square before joining the others the same night. And so the people in our dormitory began to pound and nail, as family after family slowly put up its rack again. Long after Nixon left China and arrived back in the United States, the drying racks in our dormitory had still not been completely rebuilt.

CHEN RUOXI (Chen Jo-hsi) was born in Taiwan in 1938. In the early 1960s, she studied in the U.S. In 1966, she and her husband emigrated to mainland China and lived there for the next seven years, and her experiences during that time are a source for the stories collected here. She later lived in Canada and the U.S. again before returning to Taiwan, where she currently lives. She has published thirty books in Chinese. Her other books in English include *Spirit Calling; The Old Man; The Short Stories of Chen Ruoxi;* and *Democracy Wall and the Unofficial Journals.*

HOWARD GOLDBLATT is Research Professor of East Asian Languages at the University of Notre Dame. The foremost translator of modern and contemporary Chinese literature in the West, he has translated or co-translated more than thirty novels and story collections, including *Notes of a Desolate Man; Red Poppies: A Novel of Tibet; Rice;* and *The Butcher's Wife.*

PERRY LINK is Professor of East Asian Studies at Princeton University. His many books include *The Uses of Literature: Life in the Socialist Chinese Literary System; Banyang suibi (Notes of a Semi-Foreigner); Evening Chats in Beijing: Probing China's Predicament;* and *Popular China: Unofficial Culture in a Globalizing Society* (co-edited).